PERSPECTIVES ON EQUITY AND JUSTICE IN SOCIAL WORK

To the memory of
Carl Anderson Scott, who exemplified
the Council on Social Work Education mandate
to promote social justice.

The Carl A. Scott Memorial Lecture Series,
1988–1992

PERSPECTIVES ON
EQUITY AND JUSTICE
IN SOCIAL WORK

Dorothy M. Pearson, Editor

**COUNCIL
ON SOCIAL WORK EDUCATION**

Alexandria, Virginia

TABLE OF CONTENTS

ABOUT THE EDITOR

DOROTHY M. PEARSON, PhD, is the chair of the Carl A. Scott Memorial Fund of the Council of Social Work Education, which sponsors the annual Carl A. Scott Memorial Lectures.

Dr. Pearson holds a BA (magna cum laude) in sociology from the Southern University-Baton Rouge, an MS in social work from the University of Wisconsin-Milwaukee, and a PhD in social welfare from the University of Wisconsin-Madison. Her career in social work education began at the University of Wisconsin-Milwaukee and included positions at the University of Miami School of Medicine and at the Barry University School of Social Work. She is now a full professor at the Howard University School of Social Work, where her current roles include teaching and research. At Howard, she played a major role in the planning and implementation of the doctoral program, and as such, was the first director of that program and is former associate dean of the school.

Dr. Pearson has also been the recipient of many honors, awards, and appointments, which include that of chair of the Black Social Work Educators Group and of past treasurer of the Council on Social Work Education. Her previous publications have been in the areas of mental health and women's issues.

FOREWORD

This volume is in tribute to the life and work of Carl Anderson Scott, who joined the Council on Social Work Education (CSWE) in 1968 as a senior consultant on minority groups and retired in 1985 as associate executive director. An effective champion of social justice, Mr. Scott received a BS in psychology in 1950 and an MSW in 1954 from Howard University. He joined CSWE after serving in practice and administrative positions in children and family service agencies and as director of admissions and assistant professor at the New York University School of Social Work.

Mr. Scott spearheaded CSWE's early efforts to promote human diversity in social work education by securing funding to recruit minority group students and faculty from various branches of the former U.S. Department of Health, Education, and Welfare and from private foundations. In the 1970s, his energy and expertise guided five minority task forces in developing a number of major programs to increase the number of minorities in social work education and to integrate minority content into the curriculum. With funding from the National Institute of Mental Health, Mr. Scott single-handedly developed CSWE's two minority fellowship programs, one designed to prepare mental health researchers and the other, to prepare clinicians for teaching and practice. Through these programs more than 300 African Americans, Asian Americans, Native Americans, Mexican Americans, and Puerto Ricans have received stipend support for doctoral study. To date, over 150 fellows have earned their doctorates and are providing leadership in social work education, research, and practice. The procedures Mr. Scott established in administering these programs and the process for the selection of fellows served as a model for other professional groups.

Mr. Scott's legacy lives on at CSWE and across the profession. The minority fellowship programs are among CSWE's most vibrant and highly regarded activities. Currently, forty-two fellows are engaged in doctoral study at twenty-six schools of social work. Numerous former fellows now serve as deans, directors, and faculty in schools and departments of social work. (One such former fellow is Dr. Leon F. Williams, whose 1991 Carl A. Scott Memorial lecture we present in this volume.) Others have assumed leadership positions in practice.

In recognition of Mr. Scott's contributions to CSWE and the profession, at the time of his death in 1986, the board established the Carl A. Scott Memorial Fund. Under the creative and energetic leadership of Dr. Dorothy M. Pearson, the Fund has sponsored, since 1988, a major lecture at the CSWE's Annual Program Meeting. The first five of these lectures, which are presented in this volume, follow Mr. Scott's example and represent the best of what CSWE stands for and seeks to accomplish: They contribute to the "development of knowledge, practice and service effectiveness designed to promote social justice and further community and individual well-being" (CSWE Bylaws, Article II).

We are greatly indebted to Carl A. Scott for his many lasting contributions to CSWE and social work education. We are also indebted to Dr. Pearson for her dedication to continue the spirit of his work through the Carl A. Scott Memorial Fund and the lecture series it sponsors. This volume exists only because of her gentle perseverance and hard work.

February 1993   *Donald W. Beless*
Executive Director
Council on Social Work Education

ACKNOWLEDGMENTS

The willingness of several able scholars to prepare and share their academic work at the Carl A. Scott Memorial Lectures for the past five years and the ongoing appreciation of the audience made this volume a reality. Sincere gratitude is extended to each lecturer: Dr. Leon Chestang, Dr. Dolores G. Norton, Dr. John F. Longres, Dr. Leon F. Williams, and Dr. Martha N. Ozawa.

The vision, dedication, and support of many others also made this volume possible. Soon after the death of Carl A. Scott, the board of directors of the Council on Social Work Education (CSWE) established the Carl A. Scott Memorial Fund. Dr. M. C. "Terry" Hokenstad was the president of CSWE at that time; both of his successors, Dr. Julia M. Norlin and Dr. Michael L. Frumkin continued to support the activities of this Fund. Likewise, over this time period, the executive directors, Dr. Eunice O. Shatz and Dr. Donald W. Beless, have assisted in the maintenance operations required for the Fund's growth and development. The CSWE staff (especially those in the offices of the minority fellowship program, conference and program development, and financial management), the Carl A. Scott Advisory Panel, and former colleagues and friends of Mr. Scott have been an invaluable resource. Appreciation is extended to Dr. John F. Longres, Chair of the CSWE Publications and Media Committee and to Dr. Frederic G. Reamer, Editor-in-Chief of the *Journal of Social Work Education,* for their support of this project, as well as to Marina L. Rota, Acting Managing Editor at CSWE, who had the responsibility for the design, copyediting, and production of this publication.

I also thank Linda Beebe and Lori Eatmon of the National Association of Social Workers, who graciously gave permission to reprint the articles by Leon Chestang and Dolores Norton that had been published by the association after being presented at the lectures.

The Howard University School of Social Work, my employer and Mr. Scott's alma mater, was also generous in allowing me time to pursue the development of a program that seeks to carry out Mr. Scott's legacy of working for equity and social justice for all people. And last but not least, I thank my secretary, Ms. Paulette Sellers, who gave me her unfailing cooperation, as well as my family, friends, and colleagues who have been there for me during this endeavor.

My thanks to all of you.

Dorothy M. Pearson

INTRODUCTION

Although social work is a relatively young profession, its history of professional education is very dynamic and ever changing. These changes have been influenced by several factors. Among them have been changes in educational philosophy and professional standards, in institutional structures, and in student need and interest. Within this context, for over two decades, the profession has grappled, in a very visible way, with issues regarding equity and social justice for those the profession serves. The basis for this struggle is embedded in the overall purpose of the profession, but the societal unrest evidenced in the 1960s and 1970s was probably the impetus. (The 1980s had its glaring acts of injustices as well, and the 1990s are continuing in a similar mold.)

Social workers have debated about how to bring about the change that would ensure equity and justice. According to the *New Webster's Dictionary of the English Language* (1981), the word *equity* is defined as "the quality of being fair or impartial" and *justice,* as "what is rightly due." Thus, social work has been challenged to attain a quality of fairness and impartiality that would pervade its own body politic as well as be available to its clientele in the society-at-large. The thrust for justice implies that a right to equitable treatment exists and that without it society will be adversely affected.

Various remedies have evolved over time. The Council on Social Work Education set accreditation standards that require social work education programs to include content on ethnic groups of color, women, and other groups who are systematically subjected to oppression. Moreover, the National Association of Social Workers set guidelines that mandate the inclusion of these oppressed groups in its organizational goals and activities. In addition, several of the aforementioned groups have set up professional organizations whose goals are specific to the betterment of members of the group. Furthermore, social agencies have had direct encounters with the impact of inequity and injustice on its clients and, in some instances, have instituted specialized services for the concerned groups.

Despite the many years of discussion and various actions taken, the goal of achieving equity and social justice for oppressed groups in society is not now a reality. There is much more to know and to do. It is imperative that social work educators and practitioners (including policymakers) continue to address the issues of equity and social justice. Because the majority of the profession's clientele is traditionally found among the poor and other oppressed groups, social workers need to understand how clients from these groups frequently struggle to effect a satisfactory level of social functioning. This knowledge is essential in the formulation of intervention strategies that are acceptable and appropriate to the clientele and thereby are more likely to be successful. Further, social action directed toward change on the behalf of clients is informed with appropriate knowledge. Likewise, social policy initiatives are made meaningful by such knowledge that adheres to equity and social justice.

To this end, the papers contained in this volume make unique contributions to the professional knowledge base required for bringing about the necessary and desired change for equity and social justice.

Because educational institutions have the responsibility for educating persons for practice, an opportunity exists to provide an appropriate foundation for the knowledge, values, and skills the social worker needs. The paper by Leon Chestang outlines a strategy to infuse content on racial and ethnic minorities in the curriculum, and it focuses on the instructor's role in setting the organizing framework, the organizing principle, and the organizing concepts for the course. The approach describes and illustrates how minority content is integrated and unified with the subject matter of the course through these procedures. Dr. Chestang argues for a strategy that facilitates the infusion of content on racial and ethnic minorities throughout the curriculum rather than separate courses or special class sessions.

While Dr. Chestang presents an organizing model for minority content, Dolores Norton and John Longres provide conceptual frameworks for understanding the nature of the experiences of diverse racial and ethnic groups. These contribute to the identification of appropriate organizing concepts that were called for in the Chestang model.

Norton et al. (1978) developed a conceptual framework of human behavior, termed the *dual perspective,* that put forth the notion that social group differences should be considered in making assessments in practice. In this current paper, Dr. Norton revisits the dual perspective and points out its limitations. That is, the dual perspectives calls attention to differences but does not emphasize the common human need of all persons. Dr. Norton recommends that the dual perspective should be applied within the context of an anthropological-ecological framework that highlights universality in human behavior. She illustrates this view with a report on preliminary findings from a longitudinal study of inner-city African American children. It examines the importance of the sense of time in the early socialization process and discusses how the lack of understanding of the concept of time may affect a child's functioning in the wider world.

Dr. Longres also challenges some of the earlier approaches to ethnic sensitive practice. After presenting a critical evaluation of the cultural model, he posits that when devising an ethnic sensitive approach one cannot rely solely on the concepts of cultural norms and values. He believes the cultural model is most appropriate when working with recent refugees and immigrants but less appropriate when working with people of color whose families have been in the United States for generations. Dr. Longres argues that more attention should be given to status and status differences when working with minorities of color, and he views ethnic and racial stratification as one type of status hierarchy in the United States.

It is interesting to see the ongoing revisits and critical evaluations that are being made by social work scholars, especially those contained in this series of papers dedicated to equity and social justice.

Another paper, one by Leon Williams, critiques social work's mission at the end of the century. He examines the trends in the profession and points out factors that may not contribute to the development of social work as a vehicle for social justice. In a very powerful way, Dr. Williams presents what he believes to be evidence of growing anger and resentment among the poor and disaffected and then challenges the social work profession to take a proactive stance for change. He argues that the profession needs to take a new approach to diversity, one that is defined by those people who are oppressed and at-risk. While Dr. Williams chastens social work, he expresses confidence that social work is capable of returning to its mission of fighting for social justice.

This volume concludes with a research-based paper by Martha Ozawa about inequity in income support for children. She presents statistical data that shows that the lack of a policy on income support for children has created two kinds of inequity: categorical inequity and geographic inequity. Categorical inequity involves children being treated differently, depending on their parents' attachment to the labor force. Geographic inequity involves different amounts of Aid to Families with Dependent Children (AFDC), depending on where the children live.

Based on the data, Dr. Ozawa found a striking difference in the trend in average payments under social security (categorical equity) and AFDC (geographic equity). The social security benefits for children have increased considerably over the years, while AFDC payments for children have not. She goes on to say that there is an inverse relationship between the amount of federal subsidy and the percentage of African Americans in a state. Dr. Ozawa concludes that the nation's children are treated unfairly, and she makes several recommendations for action by the federal government to minimize these inequities.

In summary, the papers by no means include all the current thoughts in the profession on this topic. These may not even be representative, but they do present interesting and dynamic perspectives worthy of the profession's serious examination. This publication would be useful for educators, practitioners, and students at all levels of social work education and other related disciplines. While these papers were presented on an annual basis over a five-year period beginning in 1988 through 1992, they continue to be timely in relation to the issues of equity and justice. The profession, as well as the United States, and various other areas around the world, still have unfinished business on the topics presented here.

REFERENCE

Norton, D. G., with Brown, E. F., Francis, E. A., Mirase, F., and Valle, R. (1978). *The dual perspective: Inclusion of ethnic minority content in social work education.* New York: Council on Social Work Education.

*This article is
the revised version of
the Carl A. Scott Memorial Lecture
presented at the 34th Annual Program Meeting,
Council on Social Work Education,
March 1988, Atlanta, Georgia.*

*It has been reprinted from
Jacobs, C., and Bowles, D. D. (Eds.), 1988,
Ethnicity and race: Critical concepts in social work (pp. 230–240).
Silver Spring, MD: National Association of Social Workers,
by permission of
The National Association of Social Workers, Inc.*

LEON W. CHESTANG, PhD, is Professor and Dean at the Wayne State University
School of Social Work.

INFUSION OF MINORITY CONTENT
IN THE CURRICULUM

Leon W. Chestang

This chapter presents a conceptual framework designed to facilitate the integration of racial and ethnic minority content into the social work curriculum. The author addresses the following three objectives: (1) relating this content to the purposes of the field of social work, (2) proposing a structure by which this content can be infused and integrated throughout the entire curriculum, and (3) designing learning experiences by which the integration can be accomplished. He focuses on three major dimensions of course construction related to the infusion of minority content: (1) the organizing framework, which outlines the structure of the body of knowledge covered by the course and clarifies how the elements are related to each other, (2) the organizing concept, which sets forth the core conceptual idea of the course, and (3) the organizing principle, which describes the relations between and among the major concepts covered in a course. Although these conceptual formulations can be useful strategies for infusing minority content, he concludes that the achievement of this goal rests on the conviction of social work educators and their willingness to integrate this content into the curriculum.

Social work educators during the past decade have grappled with a number of issues related to the integration of racial and ethnic minority content in the social work curriculum. These issues are epitomized in the furor that characterized discussions of the African American experience during the late 1960s and the early 1970s, but they reflect similar issues raised by other oppressed ethnic groups.

During the 1960s, these issues often centered on the debate about whether the African American experience offered substantive information and whether this experience should be viewed as a legitimate area of scholarly inquiry. Another debate involved the assertion that the inclusion of minority content detracted from the limited time available to teach the primary focus of a course.

Currently, many social work students are challenging the requirement that they devote attention to racial and ethnic minority content. These are important issues, and their resolution will require continuing diligence and study. Still, a sufficient and growing body of knowledge exists that can guide the pursuit of a meaningful resolution of these issues.

This chapter is premised on the belief that a strategy to facilitate the infusion of content on racial and ethnic minorities is needed. To be effective, such a strategy should relate this content to the purposes of the field of social work, propose a structure by which this content can be infused and integrated throughout the entire curriculum, and illustrate learning experiences by which this can be accomplished. Each of these objectives will be addressed, but the main focus will be on proposing a framework that promises to facilitate the integration of ethnic and minority content in social work courses, regardless of central objectives or themes.

PROFESSIONAL PURPOSE AND MINORITY CONTENT

Social work is concerned with helping people with problems of social functioning. This concept directs attention to the various contexts in which human activity occurs, including interpersonal interactions; social roles; families, institutions, such as schools, social organizations, and neighborhoods; and communities. Because the profession also is interested in the relationship between these contexts and their reciprocal influences on each other, the concept of social functioning urges social workers to understand social processes such as the origin, development, and implementation of social welfare policy and social structures such as institutions and organizations.

Social work's interest in matters such as those previously outlined is shared by members of a host of other professions. However, social work has defined a peculiar focus: it is concerned with phenomena from the point of view of people in the situation (Bartlett, 1970). Within this perspective, observations are made, concepts defined, and generalizations formulated. This idea links humans with the contexts and conditions of their lives, calling attention to the reciprocal and interactive exchanges between and among people and their environments. Because this idea suggests the significance of the meaning events have for people, it emphasizes and validates the importance of personal and group experience.

The idea of people in a situation is not only the distinctive feature of the profession's focus, but it also suggests the theoretical basis for the link between minority content and professional purpose. It provides a compelling rationale for infusing minority content throughout the social work curriculum. This perspective should defuse the debate about the substantive nature of the African American or other racial or ethnic group experience as well as the related questions about the legitimacy of these as areas of scholarly inquiry. In addition, this perspective can help to deal with students' negative attitudes toward having to devote attention to this content and provide a practical and theoretical answer to those social work educators who argue that including content on African Americans and other minorities detracts from the time available to teach the material that is the focus of the course.

In what follows, specific principles that can guide the development of courses in the five core areas of knowledge mandated by the Council on Social Work Education (CSWE) *Curriculum Policy Statement* (1983) will be addressed. The purpose of this chapter is to set forth a conceptual scheme for infusing minority content in the social work curriculum. It does not attempt in any detailed way to specify substantive content either for the knowledge area or the particular racial group used to exemplify the process. Much substantive information is available in the literature, easily accessible to the reader. It is hoped that the strategy offered in this chapter will facilitate the infusion of minority content regardless of the knowledge area or the ethnic minority group being addressed.

CONCEPTUALIZING A COURSE OF STUDY

Educators must surmount both attitudinal and intellectual barriers to integrate minority content into curricula. The attitudinal barriers were alluded to earlier and have been discussed in the literature. The discussion in combination with the mandates of CSWE (*Curriculum Policy Statement,* 1983) has resulted in significant penetration of these barriers. Similarly, significant progress has been made in resolving the intellectual impediments of infusing minority content. What remains is the development of a strategy to ensure continued progress in this area.

The strategy proposed here urges social work educators, regardless of the course being designed, to clarify and to specify three major dimensions of course construction related to the infusion of minority content. The three dimensions to be discussed in turn are: (1) the organizing framework, (2) the organizing concept, and (3) the organizing principle. This strategy rests on the assumption that conceptualizing a course involves identifying the elements of a particular area of knowledge and relating the elements to each other. Regardless of the knowledge area, these elements involve key concepts that describe, clarify, and explain the phenomenon under study. Attention to these dimensions provides a structure for infusing minority content and keeps it closely tied to the broader considerations of the course. Thus, it avoids the gratuitous quality that inevitably attends when this content is presented in one or two class meetings or when a representative of a minority group is invited to give an occasional guest lecture.

The Organizing Framework

Many social work educators conceive of core courses in social work curricula too narrowly. The bases for this tendency often are related to limitations of time, the need to cover large bodies of knowledge, and the instructor's personal interests and competencies. When it is recognized, however, that the failure to develop a sufficiently broad conceptualization of a course impedes the infusion of minority content, it is possible to take steps to move beyond these impediments. Identifying and setting forth the organizing framework of the course is a crucial step in this process of infusion.

The organizing framework is the conceptual model of the course summarizing its essential dimensions and its terrain (Figure 1). The organizing framework identifies the elements of a course at a conceptual level and tells what is to be studied. This author has noted elsewhere, for example, that the "terrain" of human behavior in the social environment must include the study of human development and the person's interaction with the environment (Norton, 1978, p. 12). Certain specific topics follow from such a study, including the development of the human life cycle, which involves people's basic needs and drives related to the life stages, and the role of the environment on the life cycle, reactions to stress, and the ways people cope.

The infusion of information on minorities requires blending information from the group's perspective on such matters as the history of the group, acculturation experiences, racial and ethnic experiences, and socioeconomic experiences. These categories are not exhaustive, but they illustrate the kind of information usually included in Human Behavior in the Social Environment (HBSE) courses. Norton (1978)

FIGURE 1. Conceptual model of the course.

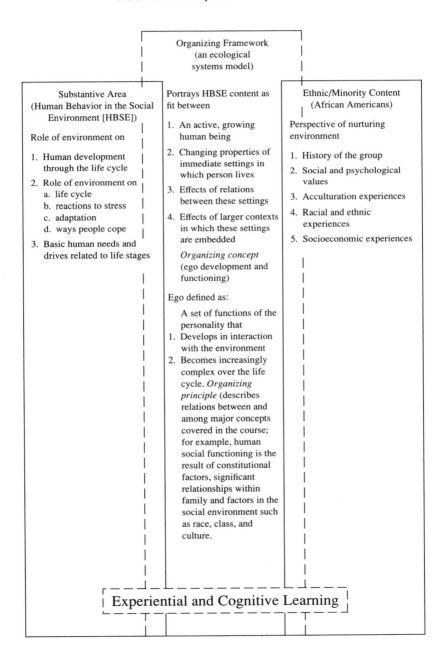

points out that for such a course to integrate minority content, knowledge about the specific ethnic group in its "nurturing environment" must be included. This content "can take many forms of organization depending on the minority or ethnic group being considered" (p. 12). The point of emphasis here, however, is that the organizing framework can provide the vehicle for linking the general course content to a specific minority or ethnic group.

The ecological systems model, an organizing framework, can be used to order minority content in human behavior courses. From this perspective, Bronfenbrenner (1979) has claimed that

> human development involves the scientific study of the progressive, mutual accommodation between an active, growing human being and the changing properties of the immediate settings in which the developing person lives, as this process is affected by relations between these settings, and by the larger contexts in which these settings are embedded. (p. 21)

As an organizing framework, this model outlines the structure of the body of knowledge covered by the course and clarifies how the elements are related to each other. Thus, the organizing framework integrates the elements and gives unity to the subject matter. Clearly, these functions provide important aids to the instructional and learning processes. From the instructor's point of view, sequencing, coherence, and increasing complexity are protected. From the student's point of view, clarity, logic, and understanding are likely. One sees these functions in operation as the student learns that people's basic needs and drives affect their motivation, adaptation, and coping. The student also recognizes that these processes are affected by the social context (environments) in which the developing person lives. As can be seen readily, content on ethnic minorities is crucial to understanding these processes. The student can then understand how one's ghetto or barrio experience or reactions to discrimination and prejudice influence adaptation.

The unity of the subject matter is underlined by the organizing framework through its portrayal of each element of course content as inextricably linked to the other; the omission of any link results in inaccuracies in understanding, gaps in knowledge, and insufficient skill. The organizing framework serves two other critical functions. First, it provides a scheme for analysis, comparison, and criticism, skills essential to the competent practice of social work and effective student learning. Second, it clarifies the difference between teaching a theory and teaching an area of study. In relation to the organizing framework, a specific theory becomes an element of the course, while the area of study usually is more inclusive, encompassing several theories. If the educator is confused on this point, he or she will focus on a single theory and compromise the comprehensiveness of an area of study (for example, psychoanalytic theory in HBSE). This not only limits the opportunity to include minority content but may block a more comprehensive view of the subject matter related to other themes as well. A human behavior course focused on psychoanalytic theory, because this subject is so broad and complex, often leaves little opportunity to consider the role of the environment on human development and social functioning. Conversely, a course using a broader organizing framework would consider psychoanalytic theory as one element to be included among many other theories of personality development. Considered in this fashion, psychoanalytic theory provides one among a number of other perspectives on personality development. What the foregoing suggests, then, is that an organizing framework is an ordering device with important consequences for the structure and content of a course as well as for the nature and kind of knowledge and skill the student is expected to acquire.

The Organizing Concept

The organizing concept sets forth the core conceptual idea of the course. It is the theme around which all other aspects of course content revolve. Throughout the course, it is examined, elaborated on, expanded, and explored. The organizing concept selected for a course, therefore, must be central to understanding the structure of an area of study, its relationship to other areas of study, and the professional purposes served by it. The organizing concept is illustrated by the concept of ego development in an HBSE course. Students must understand this concept as more than an abstraction. This requires understanding that the ego is a set of functions of the personality, that it develops in interaction with the environment, and that it becomes increasingly complex over the life cycle.

Opportunities to structure minority content into such learning are many. Students learn that there is variation in the ways in which the ego adapts, integrates, chooses, and defends itself. Further, students learn how the environment interacts with biological and cultural factors and the social structure to influence the character of ego development and operation. As the course progresses through the life stages, one can see how race and ethnicity influence ego development. Approached in this way, the infusion of minority content not only is achieved, but the student gains a fuller appreciation and understanding of the subject matter addressed in the course.

The effective use of the organizing concept can aid the inclusion of minority content in a course, but it is important that this content also be ordered so that appropriate linkages and syntheses are made. For this purpose, a separate organizing concept specifically designed for this is useful. Chestang's (1976) formulation of "duality in black culture and coping" and Norton's (1978) concept of the dual perspective are illustrative. Norton defines the dual perspective as

> the conscious and systematic process of perceiving, understanding, and comparing simultaneously the values, attitudes, and behavior of the larger societal system with those of the client's immediate family and community system. It is the conscious awareness on the cognitive and attitudinal levels of the similarities and differences in the two systems. (p. 3)

Because this perspective requires substantial knowledge and empathic appreciation of the majority system and the client's nurturing environment, it "allows one to experience each system from the point of view of the other" (p. 3).

Solomon's (1976) concept of "empowerment" also is relevant. Empowerment "refers to a process whereby persons who belong to a stigmatized social category throughout their lives can be assisted to develop and increase skills in the exercise of interpersonal influence and the performance of values social roles" (p. 6).

Either of these ideas—duality in black culture and coping, the dual perspective, or empowerment—can be used to further solidify the structure of minority content in a given social work course. These concepts, of course, are not exhaustive of the possibilities. Others that come to mind are oppression and racism. The main point here, however, is that an organizing concept specifically addressing minority content orders such content and provides a rationale for its inclusion in the course.

The Organizing Principle

The organizing principle describes the relations between and among the major concepts covered in a course. These relationships should result in a statement of the fundamental assumption or hypothesis of the body of knowledge addressed.

Consider, the example, the following organizing principle used by this author in a course titled "Race, Culture, and Social Functioning":

"Human social functioning is the result of the interaction of constitutional givens, significant relationships within the family, and factors in the social structure and social environment such as race, class, and culture." As this statement indicates, the student's attention is directed to the key dimensions of knowledge to be examined and understood in the course. The statement also contains a point of view that defines what is significant to the area of study: constitutional or biological attributes, relations in the family, and social factors that impinge on the person are important in order to understand the social functioning of African Americans. It is important to note also that the statement links these elements by hypothesizing that the interaction among them influences the quality and character of social functioning.

The statement directs the student's attention to key dimensions of knowledge and the links among them, but it does not say specifically what the nature of these connections are or how they come about. That is the function of the many subprinciples and hypotheses that will be covered in the course. The organizing principle is the grand idea of the course, serving as the anchor for the related ideas that give it vitality. It is stated at a high level of abstraction because it is intended to subsume a large body of information.

Enough has been said to show the relevance of this idea to structuring minority content into a course. It bears repeating, however, that structuring minority content into a course through an organizing principle enhances the probability that the student's understanding and application of knowledge will accurately reflect the fundamental assumption inherent in the area of study.

Before leaving this topic, it may be useful to distinguish the organizing principle from the organizing framework. The organizing framework summarizes and describes the general types of information essential to knowledge in an area of study. The organizing principle makes this knowledge concrete by moving it to a level of greater specificity. The organizing framework offers a broad outline of the subject matter; the organizing principle relates its specific elements into a coherent statement of its most fundamental assumption.

DESIGNING LEARNING EXPERIENCES
TO INFUSE MINORITY CONTENT

The organization of course content should reflect the purposes of the course. Because social work is concerned with understanding and intervening in human problems, courses ordinarily include facts, concepts, theories, and principles that bear on these matters. A major point of this chapter is that knowledge of racial and ethnic minorities is an integral component of any area of study in social work.

Techniques and approaches for ensuring the infusion of ethnic and minority content in the social work curriculum will be discussed. Two areas of learning thought to be central to the infusion will be considered: (1) attitudinal responses, and (2) substantive knowledge, including its application.

Attitudinal Responses

Although students bring a host of attitudes toward minorities from their family and life experiences, the instructor sets the tone for their attitudes toward the relevance and importance of minority content as components of professional knowledge and competence. A norm permitting open class discussion and conflict around opinions and controversial ideas among the students and between the instructor and students must be set. This means, for example, that in a course on social welfare policy, a student must be free to express the view that affirmative action results in injustices to members of the dominant society. Further, it means that the instructor must protect this student's right to have his or her say. Similarly, students holding other points of view must have the same protection and rights. The instructor's role, after ample opportunity for class discussions, is to relate these various points of view to the orientation and purposes of the profession. Again, the organizing framework, concept, and principle can be used to analyze the various points of view in relation to their fit with the accepted knowledge and perspective of the profession.

Inherent in this approach is the acceptance of controversial ideas and conflict as natural and essential aspects of learning. This especially is necessary because the material is laden with emotional, social, and personal implications. But this is not acceptance of controversy and conflict for their own sake. For attitudinal change and learning to occur, controversy and conflict must be considered in the light of professional development and competence, and the instructor must link controversy and conflict to the objectives of the course.

A brief illustration of one technique follows. In an effort to help students acquire an emotional understanding of what "taking the attitude of the other" means, this author engages them in the following experiential exercise:

Issue 1: Identify three of your most dearly held values. Prioritize these three values.

• Tell how you learned these values.
• Tell how these values are reflected in your functioning and your family's functioning.
• How has your perspective (the meaning of or ways of living out these values) changed on the application of these values?
• What values about family life do you hold which were not learned in your family?

Issue 2: What does it mean "to take the attitude of the other?"

• Identify an attitude commonly held by African American (or other ethnic group) people that you *do not* share. Be specific.
• Describe the process you would go through in order to take this attitude for yourself.

This exercise requires students to confront their values and to come to terms with their attitudes. The exercise also provides a lesson in the difficulty and the advantages of taking the attitude of the other. Through it, students move beyond cognitive self-awareness to emotional awareness of the feelings and attitudes of persons whose life experiences often are vastly different from their own.

Substantive Knowledge

It is not possible to detail what the students need to understand and intervene in the problems of the various minority groups encountered in social work. It is possible, however, to outline briefly the kinds of information relevant to the core courses students need. Knowledge of human behavior has already been alluded to in this chapter. Much of that information also is pertinent to social work practice, social welfare policy, and field instruction courses.

In addition to an analytic perspective derived from a broad organizing framework focused on the interaction between person and environment, students need specific information from a minority perspective, including, but not limited to, the work of minority scholars. It is important for students to understand the feelings, attitudes, values, and perspectives that grow out of minority group experiences including how these experiences and perspectives result in life-styles, coping strategies, world views, and attitudes. Further, these results have implications for the minority person's behavior and attitudes toward social welfare policies and programs. These factors have implications for research courses in social work. In addition, it is essential for students to appreciate and understand how the questions posed, the research designs used, and the interpretation of data affect the minority person's view that such research might contribute to or alleviate the negative valuation of minorities in society.

In the course on race and culture, it was helpful to focus the course content exclusively on theories and research that specifically address issues relevant to the black experience and areas of interest to the profession. Such issues included childhood, the role of women, the role of men, family functioning, race relations, and social intervention. By examining systematic theories and empirical research, students learn how to analyze critically their own views as well as the methodology and findings of research. They come away from the course with a clearer view of the minority experience, greater skill in assessing the negative valuation of minorities, and increased awareness of their roles in the helping process. A greater respect for the content is expressed because it is seen as more substantial than the opinions and preachments of colleagues or the instructor. Students believe that their attitudes and knowledge have been influenced by data.

Finally, the student needs an opportunity to apply learning regarding the minority experience and perspective. This can be done in both classroom learning experiences and in field instruction. In the classroom, the annotated bibliography on a specific student-selected question or issue provides an excellent opportunity to review information for the light it sheds on the question or issue raised by the student. The annotated bibliography is useful especially if the student is asked to provide a summarizing narrative that precedes or concludes the bibliography. This requires the student to become involved in the issues he or she has read about.

The term paper is a familiar device for assessing student learning. Whatever the subject area, content on minorities can be infused if the instructor explains that a comprehensive discussion of the subject must include attention to the meaning, perspective, and impact of the general issue on a particular minority group or minorities in general.

Using another technique for infusing minority content, the oral report, the student examines an issue and reports on the state of the art, findings, or conclusions. Again, the instructor expects that this dimension of the subject matter must be covered for the work to be completed. The advantage of using the oral report as an application device is that the student shares a point of view on the material and interacts with colleagues on the topic.

Field instructors are in an excellent position to help students see examples of the minority experience and perspective. As students engage clients in information gathering, and as they arrive at diagnostic assessments and plan interventive strategies, they can be helped to use their knowledge and appreciation of the minority perspective to carry out these steps in the helping process. Faculty liaisons may find it necessary to help field instructors to include this dimension in their work with students. Field instructors also should encourage students to discuss openly their reactions, including gaps in understanding, biases, and fears in work with minorities. In this way, the norm suggested for the class is carried through to the field, and the student's integration of ethnic and minority content is enhanced.

Although the relevance of minority content to education for social work is acknowledged, its infusion into the entire curriculum has proceeded with varying degrees of success. Efforts to achieve such infusion have been characterized by a disjointed approach such that minority content is taught apart from the core courses or it has been "tacked on" to a few class sessions. In other instances, it has been give an obligatory nod by inviting representatives of minority groups to present a "guest lecture."

Approaches such as these fail to achieve the educational objectives of this content, and, therefore, limit the opportunity for students to acquire the knowledge and skill necessary for competent professional practice. To reach educational objectives, a structural approach to the infusion of minority and ethnic content is proposed. This chapter has described such an approach to help educators build this content into the design of their courses. However, although the conceptual formulations discussed can become useful strategies for infusing minority content, the achievement of this goal rests on the conviction of social work educators about the relevance of this information and their willingness to strive consistently to integrate it throughout the curriculum.

REFERENCES

Bartlett, M. (1970). *The common base of social work practice.* New York: National Association of Social Workers, Inc.

Bronfenbrenner, V. (1979). *The ecology of human development.* Cambridge: Harvard University Press.

Chestang, L. W. (1976). Environmental influences on social functioning: The black experience, in P. S. J. Cafferty and L. W. Chestang (Eds.), *The diverse society: Implications for social policy.* Washington, DC: National Association of Workers, Inc.

Council on Social Work Education. (1983). *Curriculum policy statement.* New York: Council on Social Work Education.

Norton, D., with Brown, E. F., Francis, E. A., Mirase, F., and Valle, R. (1978). *The dual perspective.* New York: Council on Social Work Education.

Solomon, B. B. (1976). *Black empowerment.* New York: Columbia University Press.

*This article is
the revised version of
the Carl A. Scott Memorial Lecture
presented at the 35th Annual Program Meeting,
Council on Social Work Education,
March 1989, Chicago, Illinois.*

*It has been
reprinted from the
Journal of Social Work, 38 (1), 82–90,
by permission of the National Association of Social Workers, Inc.*

DOLORES G. NORTON, PhD, is Professor at the University of Chicago School of
Social Service Administration.

DIVERSITY, EARLY SOCIALIZATION, AND TEMPORAL DEVELOPMENT: THE DUAL PERSPECTIVE REVISITED

Dolores G. Norton

Although the dual perspective should be used to focus on diversity, it should be applied within the context of an anthropological-ecological framework to prevent stereotyping, to illuminate the universal goals of societal organization underlying human behavior, and to explore the early socialization of children. This view is illustrated with preliminary findings from an ongoing longitudinal study of lower socioeconomic inner-city African American children that examines the importance of a sense of time, its evolution in early socialization, and the relationship of parent-child interactions to the development of a sense of time.

American society is becoming ever more diverse with the increasing number of new racial and ethnic groups entering the country and the growth of traditional minority groups. By the year 2000, one in every three Americans will be in a minority group (Hodkinson, 1985). Social workers will continue to serve many of these communities. Although they need to understand group differences, a concentration on such differences often leads to pejorative views. This article suggests that social workers should use the dual perspective to focus on differences but also that they should apply this perspective within the context of an anthropological-ecological approach to emphasize the universal goals of societal organization that underlie human behavior. The author uses Geertz's (1973) concept of *mechanisms of control* to explore the early socialization of children by adults to fit into their own societies. The common goals of socialization are implemented by various societies depending on their histories and environments. However, in a diverse society such as that of the United States, socialization varies in different familial groups and does not always prepare children for life within the major society on important dimensions. The anthropological-ecological approach is illustrated by research on the temporal development of lower socioeconomic African American children, which provides a case example of the continuing need for frameworks that direct social work's attention to diversity but that consider diversity within the context of universal guidelines and the goals of societal organization.

DUAL PERSPECTIVE

In the 1970s, some social workers attempted to develop conceptual frameworks of human behavior that urged practitioners to consider social group differences in their assessment and practice (Brown, 1974; Brown & Gilbert, 1977; Chestang, 1972; Norton et al., 1978; Solomon, 1976). They surmised that a "homogenized" view of human behavior, with little awareness of the different sociocultural, socioeconomic, or racial histories of diverse American social groups, is a barrier to effective intervention based on an understanding of clients' interactions with their total environmental or ecological systems. However, other social workers questioned whether an emphasis on diversity conflicted with one of social work's basic beliefs: the concept of the common human needs of all people (Towle, 1945/1965).

The Council on Social Work Education (CSWE) bridged this difference of opinion by encouraging the development of models to understand diversity, but CSWE stressed that once effective frameworks were developed, they should be melded into cornerstone social work beliefs, practices, and courses. In support of this rationalization, CSWE sponsored a number of task forces to explore and develop content on various minority groups for use in social work education. The work of one task force focused on the potential dualism faced by minorities in the United States. The idea of dualism developed from the belief that the family and community environments of many minority groups may not match those of the larger society on all dimensions and, hence, that social workers must consider any such incongruities faced by minority clients in at least these two social systems. This concept is called the *dual perspective* (Norton et al., 1978).

Using concepts from social systems, sociology, and psychology already adopted by social work, the dual perspective posits that all people are embedded in at least two interrelated social systems: (1) that of their immediate socioeconomic, cultural, or racial environment represented by their family and community (the nurturing system of

Chestang [1972] or the microsystems of Bronfenbrenner [1979]) and (2) that of the economic, political, and educational systems of the wider society—the general social and political macrosystem. Theoretical foundations for the concept of these two systems are based on Erikson's (1968) notion that early significant others are the first purveyors of socialization within the immediate culture of the family and community system and Mead's (1974) symbolic interaction concept, which relates experiences from the wider society to how one views oneself—the idea of the generalized other. Social workers practice a dual perspective by consciously juxtaposing the reality of the family systems against that of the larger society in assessments and interventions. They do so by perceiving, evaluating, and understanding the degree of incongruence between these two systems. That is, they must continuously compare the beliefs, aspirations, and behavior that are acceptable in the client's immediate family and community systems to those that are acceptable in the larger societal social systems.

A major goal of this early framework was to prevent the a priori assignment of pathology to behavior that was functional in the client's specific family and community system but that seemed incongruent and even dysfunctional from the perspective of the larger societal system. However, as one of the earlier models for considering diversity, the concept of the dual perspective has limitations (DeHoyas, DeHoyas, & Anderson, 1986). It directs attention to cultural differences, but it has no theoretical power to engage the underlying common human needs of societal groups—a concept emphasized and valued in social work. Although the dual perspective pushes social workers to recognize diverse groups and to understand that disparities between these groups' beliefs and behavior and those of the wider society can often be explained by historical and cultural experiences such as discrimination, racism, or social and economic structural dislocation, rather than by personal pathology, the emphasis is still on differences. If pushed to explain the lack of congruence between the environment of one cultural or racial group compared to the environment of the major society, one can arrive at an explanation of inherent deficit, or blaming the victim. Hence, an emphasis primarily on differences often becomes pejorative.

ANTHROPOLOGICAL-ECOLOGICAL APPROACH

This article suggests a more neutral approach based on assumptions about the nature and organization of all human societies derived from anthropology. Geertz (1973) proposed that human culture is best seen not as complexes of concrete or discrete behavioral patterns or even traditions, but rather as a set of integrating mechanisms—plans, recipes, or rules for governing behavior—or even as a set of control mechanisms that ensure the survival of a particular society. All human societies or groups set up these control mechanisms to ensure that behavior needed for the survival of that specific society occurs. Although the content and style of these behaviors may differ, depending on the histories and needs of a particular societal group, the purposes or goals are similar. Certain patterns recur from society to society for the simple reason that the requirements they serve are generically human. Although this control-mechanism view of culture and human behavior may offend social workers on its surface, it forges a common underpinning for understanding cultural differences and demonstrates the basic plasticity of all humans to survive under varying physical and social conditions.

One such basic control mechanism common to all human societies is the set of relationships between children and adults. Most societies entrust their infants to some form of the family to socialize them. Socialization in its broadest terms is conceived as the process by which individuals become competent, participating members of a society (Schwartz, 1976), that is, the process by which adults prepare children for competent adulthood in their own social group. Human beings raise their children to fit into the society they know. Thus, child-rearing practices reflect what parents know about life in their community, what they believe will be useful, and what they recognize as realistic aspirations for their children.

This approach works fairly well when the total population within a society has a similar heritage, when economic and social norms change slowly, and when all groups in the society have relatively equal access to the society's major institutions and resources. However, in a diverse, changing society such as that of the United States, in which the history of some groups involves segregation and separation, some communities are locked in and separated from the major societal institutions and resources. They may not be entirely familiar with all the subtle nuances of the wider society; the "thick" description of society conceived by Geertz (1973) indicates an in-depth, intimate understanding of cultural meaning and behavior (see also Ryle, 1949). Children in any societal group are taught primarily what is useful in their environment. Thus, these families may not be able to teach their children all the rules and tools for success in the mainstream society. Families cannot give meaning to values they do not share or to experiences that do not exist in their environment (Norton, 1990).

Although this approach is particularly helpful in preventing stigma in understanding minority groups, its value is that it can be used to understand differences in any societal group without stigma, even those considered in the mainstream. For example, in the Infant Development Project: Children at Risk (IDP) described later, an experienced kindergarten teacher was interviewed who had recently been transferred from an inner-city school to a school in a luxurious, high-rise neighborhood. Much to her surprise, when she lined up her privileged new charges to go downstairs to the play yard, they had hardly taken two steps when they all went tumbling down the steps. Puzzled, she lined them up again and watched the same thing happen. As a veteran teacher she had encountered children with many deprivations, but she had never met any five-year-olds without a physical impairment who did not "do stairs." Observing carefully, she noticed that most of the little feet did not make the necessary motions to negotiate the stairs smoothly in rhythm with others in the line. Assuming that most five-year-olds can develop this type of locomotion, she ordered a set of play stairs for her classroom and began to teach them. In less than one month, her pupils were descending the stairs with great synchrony, as agile as any of their contemporaries.

She eventually found out that the students did not know how to go up and down stairs because they lived in high-rise apartments with elevators that always worked. Walking up and down just was not a part of their daily developmental experiences. Although occasional brushes with stairs may have occurred in visits to museums and to grandparents, they were always accomplished with the aid of a firm adult hand. On their own, without assistance, the children did not have functional competence with stairs.

The Geertzian view that child-rearing relations and behavior between adults and children are universal control mechanisms to ensure the survival of the society is helpful here. The notion that all human families raise their children to fit into the society they know forces the intervener to look beyond pejorative explanations of difference. Without the knowledge that some lack of experience may prevent children from negotiating stairs at age five, the teacher might have labeled the children pejoratively. Instead, she ferreted out the problem and devoted extracurricular attention to ameliorating it. In the inner city, the children might have been labeled *disadvantaged* because they were not exposed to a practice that is common in the wider society: descending stairs. Even worse, they may have been labeled *deficient* in their ability to negotiate stairs, and nothing would have been done about it.

SOCIAL CONSTRUCTION OF MEANING AND ECOLOGY

Before discussing socialization and temporal development, one needs to consider another concept that embraces notions from social psychology, personality theory, and anthropology: the epistemology of social cognition, or inquiry into how people use the ecology of their environment to construct meaning for themselves based on their experiences. Children who are immersed in the environment of their families and neighborhoods begin to build on their perceptions about their world and gradually construct what is reality to them. The content of that construction is determined by their own personalities in interaction with their social, physical, linguistic, historical, and cultural experiences determined primarily by their families. The children extract information from these experiences at all levels and organize it into schemas that are consistent with their personalities. These schemas help them make sense out of the environment. The process is both interdependent and circular, with the environment and the individual influencing each other. This construction of meaning largely determines the children's behavior.

Social work has long been interested in understanding the individual in relation to his or her total environment and has turned to the ecological model as one framework to do so (Bronfenbrenner, 1979, 1986; Brower, 1988; Germain, 1987; Norton & Kivnick, forthcoming; Whittaker, Schinke, & Gilchrist, 1986). This article combines the anthropological approach just described with a discussion of early socialization and the construction of meaning to examine temporal development in children.

INFANT DEVELOPMENT PROJECT

The anecdote on one group of children's inexperience with stairs illustrates that early life in various familial groups in a pluralistic society may not teach children how to fit into all dimensions of the larger society. The inability to climb and descend stairs is not costly for the children. The longitudinal research on low-income, inner-city African

American children from birth through first grade described here seeks more subtle and costly examples of differences between what children learn in their early environment and the requirements of the larger society.

Guided by the anthropological framework, IDP is an ongoing attempt to document, describe, and understand the early environment and developmental experiences of the children. It uses a modified ethnographic approach to understand life from the viewpoints and perspectives of the people being studied (Hymes, 1974). The focus is on the children's natural environment to describe more precisely the patterns of interactions and experiences that shape their lives. Data were collected by videotaping mothers and babies in the hospital the second day after birth, followed by videotaping in the home at regular intervals as frequently as every six weeks the first two years, every three months until age three, and every six months thereafter. The children are now nine years old. The camera focuses continuously on the target baby or child, recording all interactions. The mothers are told to continue their activities as if the videotaper were not there. Additional data include the mothers' life, medical, and employment histories; social and cognitive tests on both the mothers (Wechsler Adult Intelligence Scale [Alpern, Boll, & Shearer, 1984]) and the children (the McCarthy Scales of Children's Abilities [McCarthy, 1972] at ages three and six); transcripts of off-camera activities; and rich data on a variety of family activities observed during the frequent tapings. Providing continuous natural data during a period when the children grow rapidly and acquire intellectual and social skills, the tapes can be stopped and observed repeatedly so that various techniques of analysis can be used and many variables can be examined. The ultimate goal of the project is to use such information to develop appropriate models of family-support intervention and school curricula that are based on what is meaningful and thus effective in a particular community located in a complex and diverse society.

Sample

Designed to study minority children whose social and physical environment puts them at the highest risk for incongruence with the mainstream, the study sought young mothers who did not live with older family members, whose education did not go beyond high school at the birth of the target baby, and who lived in census tracts that were below the metropolitan median in per capita income and housing value and above the median in rates of housing density, transience, vacant housing, crime, and neonatal mortality. Mothers giving birth in one of two major metropolitan hospitals during the three months of collecting the sample who met the study criteria were asked to participate. Thirty-seven out of 41 mothers who met the criteria agreed to participate, and 26 (70 percent) remain in the study after nine years. Attrition is due primarily to moves out of state, moves within the city without informing the project of the change of address, and one death of a child from jaundice at age 10 months. The mothers' mean age was 21.3 years when they entered the study, but all except one are considered adolescent mothers because they were teenagers at the birth of their first child.

Unique in the frequency of observations and length of study, this research makes it possible to observe the evolution of the children in critical areas of social and cognitive development. This article reports only on the children's development of a sense of time. The rest of the article explores the universal meaning of time, examines individual child-family interactional patterns associated with the development of a sense of time, and discusses the relation between the development of a sense of time and early school experiences—the children's first independent foray into the larger society.

Importance of Time in People's Lives

Definition of Time. The development of a sense of time is a more important and subtle factor in socialization than is the ability to climb stairs. How important is the concept of time? Although there is an increasing literature on the developmental psychology of time cutting across several disciplines, social work has not used it to understand human behavior. This literature stresses that time is an integral and basic component of all human life—that all human beings need a temporal framework within which to act, think, and relate to the world around them. An understanding of the continuity of time helps people place themselves within and order their world. Beyond clocks and calendars, time is the temporal organization of experiences based on the awareness of change (Campbell, 1986; Fraisse, 1964; Fraser, 1989; Friedman, 1982; Kant, 1781/1956; Michon, 1990; Michon, Pouthas, & Jackson, 1988; Newton, 1687/1971; Piaget, 1969; Plato, 1965). Humans observe changes as day fades into night and children grow. They note these changes, store them in their memories, integrate them into logical sequences, and make premises about the future based on their understanding of the succession of events. They can then order their behavior by those premises. Understanding the succession of events establishes the potential of ordering one's behavior at one point in time to have control and efficacy regarding some desired outcome at a future point (Gorman & Weissman, 1977). Thus, expectations and plans are set up on the basis of the organization of temporal experience (Michon et al., 1988).

Time and a Sense of Self. Some theorists connect temporal development with the sense of self. The sequencing of time through the past, present, and future is called *linear time.* Understanding linear time permits us to erect a meaningful and coherent framework for living that is integrated within a core self that is consistent throughout our past and future and guides our behavior in our present environment (Brockelman, 1985; Michon & Jackson, 1985; Ricoeur, 1981). This meaningful structure of personal time relies on unifying the past, present, and future in mental and narrative discourse within a consistent sense of self (Gorman & Weissman, 1977). Relating our past, present, and future consolidates our sense of who we are and what we may become. In this meaningful narrative based on our coherent personal history, we recognize our self. Temporal order relies on "the ability to file our memories coherently" (Michon et al., 1988, p. 46). The sameness of identity in different instances over time is key to the sense of self (Melges, 1990). Thus, a firm sense of self is associated with a feeling of continuity from the past, through the present, and toward the future. If strategies for processing temporal information are not developed in early childhood or are not available in old age as a result of organic or mental disorder, distortions of the experience of time will occur that will affect the sense of self (Michon et al., 1988). The recent interest of clinical researchers in narrative and autobiographical memory supports this constructionist view of self or personal identity (Cohler, 1988; Sarbin, 1986; Shotter & Gergen, 1989).

Seriation and the Early Development of a Sense of Time. Children must understand the concept of *seriation,* the ordering of events in a temporal sequence, before they can develop an understanding of the past, present, and future—the linear model of time favored in Western society (Harner, 1982). Seriation involves the child's retention of the temporal order of behavior and sounds in memory that leads to "the ability to file our memories coherently" and permits the relative ordering of events through time. How do mothers begin to pass on ideas of the past, present, and future to their children?

Children begin to develop seriation in early sensorimotor interaction with their families in daily child care routines. In these interactions, they and their caretakers take turns as they gaze at one another, coo in preverbal vocalization, and engage in nurse-pause-play-nurse-again patterns of feeding (Kaye, 1977; McGrath & Kelly, 1986; Stern, 1977; Tronick, Als, & Brazelton, 1986). The increasing synchrony of this responsive sequential turn-taking behavior fosters the infant's awareness of change and moves toward the development of seriation.

Language is particularly important in developing seriation and the notions of past, present, and future. Individuals can share the present without language by observing some event and simultaneously sharing it with as much similarity as their personal perspectives will permit. However, the past and present have no common, visible, external reality and can be shared only through verbal language or some recorded communication. Language enhances the capacity for extending time into the past and future (Brockelman, 1985). Parents share the past and future with their children through such early statements about time as "wait," "yesterday," "tomorrow," and "now" and verb tenses indicating the past, present, and future. Thus, parents lay the foundation for understanding the linear notions of the past, present, and future, both behaviorally and cognitively.

The type of time language used is also important. Within the categories of past, present, and future, the literature defines two major types of time: physical and social (Augustine, 1953; Friedman, 1982; Kant, 1781/1956; Lewis & Weigert, 1981; McGrath & Kelly, 1986; Newton, 1687/1971). Physical time (or objective time) is more quantitative and is measured in units (such as hours, weeks, years) that are reasonably universal. Social time (or subjective time) is more qualitative, less universal, and measured in relation to particular social situations, events, and people. The social context determines the time; for example, "We will eat after I finish" or "He left when Granny came."

Although individual traits of memory and perception, combined with intelligence and personality, help organize the development of a sense of time, the type of time sense that children develop is a cognitive construction that is dependent on culture, intelligence, environmental circumstances, daily experiences, and even deliberate teaching (Campbell, 1986). Obviously, these factors are determined by the familial environment in which children are reared. Each societal group has its own temporal environment based on its rhythm and orientation, history, location, social and cultural processes, and goals. Understanding physical time is particularly critical in a modern, highly technological society such as that of the United States, in which much of the organization of economic and social behavior depends on a commonly understood location of events and procedures in time and in which a highly developed sense of self is necessary to operate in a complex world where norms change rapidly. Societal subgroups within the general culture may hold different conceptions of time or may not even be aware of all the nuances of the common conception of time (McGrath & Kelly, 1986). Thus, some families may not prepare their children to operate in the wider society on certain dimensions of time, even though the children function temporally in the immediate social and physical environment of their families.

Thus, children first establish a temporal relationship with their environment through synchronous, early sensorimotor and temporal linguistic interactions with the significant adults in their lives. In these interactions, they develop the concept of seriation that is basic to understanding the linear temporal model of the past, present, and future. They then use seriation to organize their experiences sequentially and to construct meaning historically. Thus, they gradually develop a coherent consistent identity through time that becomes recognizable as the self. The use and type of time language (social and physical) are embedded in children's early socialization and contribute to the type of temporal sense the children develop. All these processes develop in interaction with the particular culture and societal environment in which the children are reared, which may not match the dominant temporal perspectives of the major society.

Relevant IDP Findings

In some of the homes of IDP participants, little or no routine has been observed in the early lives of the children. Often these children's mothers do not work or have anyplace to go and thus have little reason to plan or observe time. The children get up whenever they awaken and then wander out to the living room, where they alternately watch television or play for the full four-hour taping. The day flows by on a seemingly unscheduled basis, unrelated to any overall division of time. Meals are sometimes prompted by someone bringing in food, the arrival of an older sibling from school asking for food, or the whining insistence of a child. Some of these mothers are too needy or too anxious to respond to their children in sensitive synchrony, as with one six-week-old who cried unattended for 28 minutes and was finally solaced with a propped bottle.

On the other hand, some mothers provide a different temporal atmosphere for their children. One mother discussed anniversaries and birthdays while baking a cake with her children; another talked about her hopes for her daughter's future and tried to provide her children with a better education by volunteering to serve daily lunch at a local Catholic school in return for free preschool enrollment; and another played peeka-boo through a box with her daughter, taking turns and setting up the alternating synchrony needed to develop seriation.

Seriation. One of the most important IDP findings was the statistically significant positive relationship between the number of time statements the mothers made to their children and the children's scores on seriation on the McCarthy Scales of Children's Abilities at age three. Using a small sample of 16 children for which all data were available, the project found that children whose mothers spoke to them more about time in daily conversations tended to rank higher on seriation measures than did children whose mothers talked less to them about time ($r = .54$, $p < .05$, see Table 1). Children who scored in the top quartile in seriation had a mean of 10.8 time statements directed to them from their mothers, compared to the mean of 3.4 time statements for the other children. Thus, children whose mothers spoke to them more about time seemed to be developing more of a sense of time at age three than did those who heard fewer time statements.

Another important IDP finding was the significant relationship between the children's seriation scores and the mothers' statements to them regarding physical time. Children whose mothers talked to them using the quantitative, objective units of physical time tended to score higher on seriation. The mothers whose children scored in the highest quartile made considerably more physical time statements to their children (mean = 4.3) than did those whose children scored lower (mean = .2). Thus, children whose mothers talked to them using physical time statements were indeed developing more of a time sense than were children who heard fewer physical time statements. However, although children who scored the highest on seriation heard more physical time statements than did the other children, all the children heard more social time statements than physical time statements. Because physical time is the primary time language used in the United States and is the time language of school, children who are exposed and socialized early to physical time may be better prepared for school than may children who hear primarily social time statements.

Despite the importance of talking about time and the children's scores on seriation, less than 2 percent of all the mothers' language to

TABLE 1. *Children's Seriation Scores, by Mother's Total Statements*
and Time Statements (N = 16)

	Seriation Scores	Total Statements	Total Time Statements	Physical Time Statements	Social Time Statements
	8	660	8	1	7
	8	452	11	4	7
	8	394	17	9	8
	8	191	7	3	4
	7	244	4	0	4
	7	496	13	0	13
	6	333	4	0	4
	6	192	1	0	1
	6	60	0	0	0
	6	54	2	1	1
	5	293	4	0	2
	5	174	4	0	4
	4	221	1	0	1
	3	128	0	0	0
	3	60	0	0	0
	2	417	8	1	7
Mean	5.8	273.3	5.2	1.3	3.9
SD	1.9	168.7	4.9	2.3	3.6

Note: Seriation by total time statements, $r = .54$, $p < .05$; seriation by physical time statements, $r = .53$, $p < .05$.

the target children included statements about time. Hence, many of these children may not be developing an understanding of the past, present, and future and thus may not be able to translate the time statements made by teachers and order their behavior by them. For example, when a teacher says, "Sit down now and finish your coloring and then you can watch the gerbils during free time," children are cued to order their behavior in the present to bring about the desired activity in the future. The children translate the statement to mean "Finish this drawing quickly, so I can play with the gerbils." This ability to translate time language is important to children who are entering the world of formal schooling.

Although the IDP has not yet formally compared the children's sense of self to their development of a sense of time, a preliminary analysis reveals that the mothers of children who tested well on the time measurements seemed to have a better sense of self-efficacy and control than did the other mothers: "These mothers were more future oriented: they voiced plans, challenged personnel in renting offices, and refused to let the public assistance office change their family health services to a new [health maintenance organization] system until they found out about the services to be offered" (Norton, 1990, p. 5). From the videotapes, these mothers also appear to be establishing early synchrony with their children. The mother of one child who scored in the highest group on seriation was finally able to leave the abusive father, swear out a peace bond, and move to a shelter.

The study of the link between a developing sense of time and functioning in the wider world is relatively new. For example, researchers in several countries are now exploring the relationship between the early temporal home environment and children's use of time to order their behavior at school (Ben-Baruch, Bruno, & Horn, 1987; Brice-Heath, 1984; Farran, 1982; Leigh, 1986). They agree that in multiethnic, multicultural societies that are undergoing rapid social change, such as those of the United States and Israel, some children's concepts of time may not match those of the school, and this lack of congruence correlates with how the children succeed in school.

IMPLICATIONS

The development of a sense of time is one example of the complex issues in understanding differential socialization and illustrates the continuing challenge to social workers to become aware of the differences in socialization and the subsequent worldview of the populations they serve. The findings on the development of a sense of time reported here are preliminary and need further study. However, they may have implications for changes in curricula that will build on what the children bring to school and give them a chance to succeed. The structure of classrooms in the early grades may need to be changed to decrease or eliminate time slots. Although social work has not used temporal development in assessment and intervention, earlier studies (Gesell & Ilg, 1946) suggested that the lack of a temporal orientation may be a handicap that has not received sufficient attention. Judgments about time have been associated with the development of a sense of self and with different aspects of school learning. For example, Piaget (1969) argued that an awareness of time releases children from egocentric views and frees them to learn about the larger world. Other early studies

(Greenberg-Edelstein, 1971) showed that difficulty learning to read was associated with temporal problems.

Ethnographic studies of specific populations like that of IDP meet social work's need to provide data to understand the experiences of different groups. Comparing children in a demographically and culturally homogeneous population who live under similar socioeconomic conditions forces the researcher and intervener to go beyond the structural variables of class and race as exclusive explanatory factors of developmental outcomes. Understanding differences in the same population may be more helpful in devising programs and policies that are responsive to the worldview and environmental press of the group than may basing the programs on norms from another group. Knowledge of the early experiences of the children from the same racial and socioeconomic background who succeed in school can be used to help those who face similar circumstances but do not succeed.

Social workers' efforts to intervene on behalf of minorities need to be based on an understanding of the construction of meaning in the people's lives, not on external perceptions. It is a major challenge to ferret out these groups' worldviews and to create effective, responsible, valid policies and programs. In accepting this challenge and responsibility, social workers borrow from other academic disciplines to discover and comprehend factors that range from the inability to climb stairs to the development of a sense of time. The search for meaning in another cultural context is complex. However, social workers have no choice, because theirs is a profession whose activities can extend from contemplating the epistemology of knowledge among different groups to applying that knowledge in gritty street-level interventions in poverty-ridden neighborhoods.

REFERENCES

Alpern, G. E., Boll, T. J., & Shearer, M. (1984). *Wechsler Adult Intelligence Scale.* Los Angeles: Western Psychological Services.

Augustine. (1953). *Confessions.* Translated by V. J. Burke. New York: Fathers of the Church. (Original was written circa 300.)

Ben-Baruch, E., Bruno, J. E., & Horn, L. L. (1987). Dimensions of time use attitudes among middle-high SES students. *Social Behavior and Personality, 15,* 1–12.

Brice-Heath, S. B. (1984). *Ways with words.* New York: Cambridge University Press.

Brockelman, P. (1985). *Time and self: Phenomenological explorations.* New York: Crossroad.

Bronfenbrenner, U. (1979). *The ecology of human development.* Cambridge: Harvard University Press.

Bronfenbrenner, U. (1986). Ecology of the family as a context for human development research perspectives. *Developmental Psychology, 22,* 723–742.

Brower, A. M. (1988). Can the ecological model guide social work practice? *Social Service Review, 62,* 411–428.

Brown, E. F., & Gilbert, B. (1977). *Social welfare practice with American Indians: A schema for the inclusion of American Indian content into the social work curriculum.* Tempe: Arizona State University School of Social Work.

Brown, E. G. (1974). *Integrating minority content into social work education.* Salt Lake City: University of Utah School of Social Work.

Campbell, J. (1986). *Winston Churchill's afternoon nap: Inquiry into the human nature of time.* New York: Simon & Schuster.

Chestang, L. (1972). *Character development in a hostile environment.* Chicago: University of Chicago Press.

Cohler, B. J. (1988). The human studies and the life history. *Social Service Review, 62,* 552–575.

DeHoyas, G., DeHoyas, A., & Anderson, C. B. (1986). Sociocultural dislocation: Beyond the dual perspective. *Social Work, 31,* 61–67.

Erikson, E. H. (1968). *Identity, youth and crisis.* New York: W. W. Norton.

Farran, D. C. (1982). Mother-child interaction, language development, and the school performance of poverty children. In L. Feagans & D. C. Farran (Eds.), *The language of children in poverty* (pp. 269–271). New York: Academic Press.

Fraisse, P. (1964). *The psychology of time.* London: Eyre & Spottiswode.

Fraser, J. T. (1989). The many dimensions of time and mind. In J. T. Fraser (Ed.), *The study of time* (Vol. 6, pp. 1–14). Madison, CT: International Universities Press.

Friedman, W. J. (Ed.). (1982). *The developmental psychology of time.* New York: Academic Press.

Geertz, C. (1973). *The interpretation of cultures.* New York: Basic Books.

Germain, C. B. (1987). Human development in contemporary environments. *Social Service Review, 61,* 565–580.

Gesell, A., & Ilg, F. L. (1946). *The child from five to ten.* New York: Harper & Bros.

Gorman, B. S., & Weissman, A. E. (1977). *The personal experiences of time.* New York: Plenum Press.

Greenberg-Edelstein, R. R. (1971). Time perception as related to reading achievement. *Journal of Perceptual and Motor Skills, 33,* 899–905.

Harner, L. (1982). Talking about the past and the future. In W. J. Friedman (Ed.), *The developmental psychology of time* (pp. 141–169). New York: Academic Press.

Hodkinson, H. L. (1985). *All one system: Demographics of education—Kindergarten through graduate school.* Washington, DC: Institute for Educational Leadership.

Hymes, D. (1974). *Foundations in sociolinguistics: An ethnographic approach.* Philadelphia: University of Pennsylvania Press.

Kant, I. (1956). *Critique of pure reason.* Translated by N. K. Smith. London: Macmillan. (Original work published 1781.)

Kaye, K. (1977). Toward the origin of dialogue. In H. R. Schaffer (Ed.), *Studies in mother-infant interaction* (pp. 89–117). London: Academic Press.

Leigh, J. P. (1986). Accounting for tastes: Correlates of risk and time preferences. *Journal of Keynesian Economics, 9,* 17–31.

Lewis, J. D., & Weigert, A. J. (1981). The structures and meanings of social time. *Social Forces, 60,* 432–462.

McCarthy, D. (1972). *McCarthy Scales of Children's Abilities.* Cleveland, OH: Psychological Corporation.

McGrath, J. E., & Kelly, J. R. (1986). *Time and human interaction.* New York: Guilford Press.

Mead, G. H. (1974). *Mind, self and society from the standpoint of a social behaviorist.* Chicago: University of Chicago Press.

Melges, F. T. (1990). Identity and temporal perspective. In R. A. Block (Ed.), *Cognitive models of psychological time* (pp. 255–266). Hillsdale, NJ: Lawrence Erlbaum Associates.

Michon, J. A. (1990). Implicit and explicit representations of time. In R. A. Block (Ed.), *Cognitive models of psychological time* (pp. 37–58). Hillsdale, NJ: Lawrence Erlbaum Associates.

Michon, J. A., & Jackson, J. L. (1985). *Time, mind, and behavior.* Berlin: Springer-Verlag.

Michon, J. A., with Pouthas, V., & Jackson, J. L. (Eds.). (1988). *Gayau and the idea of time.* Amsterdam: North Holland.

Newton, I. (1971). *Principia.* Translated by A. Motten. Berkeley: University of California Press. (Original work published 1687.)

Norton, D. G. (1990). Culturally and ecologically relevant research as a guide to support for families. *Zero to Three, 14,* 1–8.

Norton, D. G., with Brown, E. F., Brown, E. G., Francis, E. A., Mirase, F., & Valle, R. (1978). *The dual perspective: Inclusion of ethnic minority content in social work education.* New York: Council on Social Work Education.

Norton, D. G., & Kivnick, H. (forthcoming). *The dual perspective revisited: An ecological systems approach.* Alexandria, VA: Council on Social Work Education.

Piaget, J. (1969). *The child's conception of time.* London: Routledge & Kegan Paul.

Plato. (1965). *Timaeus.* Translated by H. P. Lee. Baltimore: Penguin Books. (Original work written circa 360 B.C.)

Ricoeur, P. (1981). *Hermeneutics and the human sciences.* Cambridge: Cambridge University Press.

Ryle, G. (1949). *The concept of mind.* New York: Hutchinson's University Library.

Sarbin, T. R. (1986). *Narrative psychology: The storied nature of human conduct.* New York: Praeger.

Schwartz, T. (Ed.). (1976). *Socialization as cultural communication.* Berkeley: University of California Press.

Shotter, J., & Gergen, K. (Eds.). (1989). *Texts of identity.* London: Sage Publications.

Solomon, B. (1976). *Black empowerment.* New York: Columbia University Press.

Stern, D. (1977). *The first relationship.* Cambridge, MA: Harvard University Press.

Towle, C. (1965). *Common human needs* (rev. ed.). Silver Spring, MD: National Association of Social Workers. (Original work published 1945.)

Tronick, E. Z., Als, H., & Brazelton, T. B. (1986). Monadic phases: A structural descriptive analysis of infant-mother face to face interaction. *Merrill-Palmer Quarterly, 26,* 3–24.

Whittaker, J. K., Schinke, S. P., & Gilchrist, L. D. (1986). The ecological paradigm in child, youth, and family services: Implications for policy and practice. *Social Service Review, 60,* 483–503.

*This article is
the revised version of
the Carl A. Scott Memorial Lecture
presented at the 36th Annual Program Meeting,
Council of Social Work Education,
March 1990, Reno, Nevada.*

*It has been
reprinted from the
Journal of Multicultural Social Work, 1 (1), 41–56,
by permission of The Haworth Press, Inc.*

JOHN F. LONGRES, PhD, is Professor at the University of Wisconsin-Madison School
of Social Work.

TOWARD A STATUS MODEL OF ETHNIC SENSITIVE PRACTICE

John F. Longres

Ethnic sensitive models of practice emphasize the importance of culture and cultural differences. In this article, the author describes and critically evaluates the cultural model; this model is most appropriate when working with recent refugees and immigrants but less appropriate when working with people of color whose families go back generations in the United States. He concludes that ethnic sensitive models should pay more attention to the importance of status and status differences when working with minorities of color.

During the past decade and a half, social workers have been struggling to develop models of face-to-face practice that are sensitive to the needs of people from diverse ethnic and racial backgrounds. An increasingly rich literature has emerged and as a result ethnic sensitive models of practice are being formulated and taught as keys to effective service delivery.

The most common theme within this ethnic sensitive literature is that of culture and cultural differences. Culture is a difficult concept to define but here it is defined as a set of group-based norms and values exhibited in the attitudes, beliefs, and behavioral inclinations of individual group members. Culture is not used interchangeably with ethnic and racial group or simply with group. Pluralist societies, such as that of the United States, may be composed of a number of distinct ethnic and racial groups that do not necessarily differ in norms and values.

THE CULTURAL MODEL

From the point of view of what might be called *the cultural model of ethnic sensitive practice,* effective service delivery across ethnic and racial groups is difficult because helper and client, when they are from groups with different value systems, operate from opposing meanings about the world and the way it operates. Socialization within ethnic and racial groups, it is assumed, leads clients to identify with a unique set of values that show up in the way they understand their private troubles and seek help. Helping professionals, being from a different ethnic experience and being trained within the norms of social welfare as an institution in contemporary society, also identify with a unique set of values that show up in the way they assess troubles and offer help. When helper and client come together to deal with the troubles of the client, they therefore have different understandings of why those troubles exist and different expectations of what to do about them. The likelihood that the two will talk past each other is high; liking, trust, and respect—the necessary ingredients in the helping process—become lost in a sea of miscommunication. Resistance sets in. Clients come late, miss appointments, and eventually drop out of service. In short, service delivery fails.

Contributions of the Cultural Model

The work of de Anda (1984), Green (1982), and McNeely and Badami (1984) are exemplary and will be used here to clarify the cultural model and its contributions. Their writing will also serve to illustrate the limitations of the cultural model that will be taken up in the next part of the paper.

de Anda (1984) is interested in how ethnic socialization affects psychosocial well-being and offers a rich set of what may be considered definitive implications for practice across culturally different groups. She begins by asserting there are vast, cultural differences between the United States majority culture and the culture of African, Hispanic, and Asian Americans. She goes on to argue that minority clients experience troubles in achieving psychosocial well-being because they have not been socialized into the norms of both the majority and the minority cultures. Only when they are bicultural can they expect to achieve success. For this to occur, minority people need to become bilingual; be exposed to models, mediators and translators who can instruct and point the way; be given corrective feedback as they attempt to put into practice the expectations of the dominant culture; and acquire analytic problem solving skills to meet the everyday crises of life in the larger social environment. She adds that all this is facilitated if the minority person has the racial features of the dominant group.

Green (1982) is interested in how culturally based perceptual processes affect the help seeking behavior of racial and ethnic minorities in
the United States. He gives examples of the unique cognitive maps of
Native Americans, Hispanics, African Americans, and Vietnamese
and suggests how, unless social workers are sensitive to them, these
maps may jeopardize effective service delivery. He notes, for instance,
that Anglo helpers and Native American clients have very different
understanding of alcohol use and abuse. Anglo helpers see excessive
drinking as a sign of disease or of personal weakness. Native Americans, on the other hand, see excessive drinking as a legitimate way of
participating in community ceremonies. Similarly, he notes that Anglos and Hispanics have very different ways of understanding health
and illness. Anglos use a biomedical or scientific model, while Hispanics recognize a series of disease categories based on medieval Euro-
pean and pre-Columbian indigenous tradition. As a result, Hispanic
clients will ignore medical terminology and refer to diseases as *mal ojo,
empacho,* or *susto.* They will also reject the services of physicians in
favor of *curanderos.* African Americans, he believes, also have unique
ways of understanding health and illness that have roots in old Euro-
pean and African sources. They distinguish natural from unnatural
illnesses. Natural illness results from improper care of the body, while
unnatural illness results from evil influences. For unnatural illnesses
they are likely to turn not to physicians but to psychics, "rootworkers,"
and conjurors or witches. Asian immigrants from Vietnam will have
great difficulty accepting the welfare services provided in the United
States, because they have little tradition of public welfare and attach
considerable stigma to the kinds of problems that social workers are
trained to resolve.

McNeely and Badami (1984) are interested in the way culturally
based communication styles interfere with the process of giving help.
They argue that establishing a helping relationship is difficult in interracial school settings because lower-class black youth who reside in
northern inner-city areas operate from cultural beliefs and values that
are different from their white counterparts and, by extension, from
their white social workers. Anglo American culture leads white lower-
class youth to make continuous eye contact with others, prefer the use
of first names, be emotionally cool, bashful, trustful, and learn from
books rather than actual life experiences. African American culture, on
the other hand, leads lower class youth to make intermittent eye contact, prefer the use of titles and surnames, be emotionally hot, boastful
(although not braggart), distrustful, and learn from direct experience.

Limitations of the Cultural Model

These examples demonstrate the contributions made by the cultural model to issues in relationship, assessment and intervention; social workers must be aware of the different, culturally based, world views that motivate clients and they must be willing to take on the task of promoting biculturation. The contributions made by the cultural model are real yet it will be argued that an ethnic sensitive approach cannot rely solely on the concepts of cultural norms and values. In particular, it will be argued that the cultural model fits some cross group transactions better than others. It fits best when helping newly arrived refugees and immigrants. It fits less well when helping individuals and families from groups who have been in the United States for many generations yet still experience minority status. For these, other kinds of group differences, differences not sufficiently articulated in the cultural model, become central to the helping process.

Before proceeding some clarification needs to be made. The first has to do with the meaning of minority status. It should not be assumed that all new groups coming into a society are or will become minority groups. Sociologists are in agreement that minority status is not a matter of the size of a group, differences in ethnicity or race per se, nor newness in a society. It is only when ethnic and racial stratification is taken into account that minority and majority can be distinguished. Minority and majority status has to do with the relative power, privilege, advantage and general prestige of groups within society. Minority groups are those who, over the course of their history within a particular society, emerge with limited power, privilege, and prestige and whose members, as a result, experience devaluation and disadvantage.

Second, in arguing that the cultural model is most applicable to new groups within a society, I am not invoking an assimilationist point of view. I fully endorse the ideal of biculturation embodied in the cultural model. I do believe, however, that the longer people and their families are in a society, the more they will be able to think, feel and behave according to the dominant cultural norms. Ethnicity increasingly becomes an identity, an allegiance to a group and its history, rather than a holding on to a unique set of beliefs, attitudes and behavioral inclinations. Furthermore, it is at the point at which people accept the fact of their Americanization that concerns about minority status come to the fore. The "hyphenated" American starts to wonder: "What is the place of my ethnic group of origin, and consequently my own place, within this society with which I have come to identify?"

Third, as I attempt to challenge the preeminence of the cultural model in working with minority clients, I in no way wish to eliminate it. I simply wish to argue that once minority status is taken into account other concepts besides culture and cultural values become more central to understanding help seeking behavior and in providing help.

Helping Refugees

The cultural model is best suited for helping refugees. Refugees enter the United States through displaced persons programs and, because of the history of these programs, largely come from countries with socialist economies and totalitarian political systems. In the case of refugees from Indochina and Central America, they are also likely to come from developing agricultural or industrializing nations. With refugees it is fair to assume that large cultural differences exist between their ethnic traditions and those of the United States. Green's (1982) acknowledgment that Vietnamese refugees are likely to have no experience with a welfare system, even to the point of stigmatizing the kinds of needs it aims to fulfill, makes sense. Refugees are forced involuntarily, often in a very short span of time, out of their homelands and into the United States. Their psychosocial well-being clearly depends on their ability to biculturate and social service workers of necessity become bicultural socializing agents. It is not surprising that Handelman (1983) writes the following about working with refugees and immigrants:

> The primary role of the caseworker in resettlement work is that of socializing agent. . . . A current dilemma that affects the worker's role results from the recent shift in our own cultural ideology away from the concept of the melting pot toward a notion of cultural pluralism. The worker's task is to help the immigrants or refugees adapt to their new country while maintaining their cultural and ethnic identity. (p. 3)

When insensitive helpers ignore cultural traditions or force assimilation in providing services to refugees, communication does break down and hostility is likely to occur. This was seen when the newly arrived Vietnamese went through resettlement services; they complained bitterly that their American helpers were undermining their cultural values and traditions, namely, they were undermining extended kin ties and the status of adult males, and they were teaching children to question the authority of parents (Bowen Wright, 1980).

It is also clear that when working with new refugees, the programs and service delivery suggestions made by de Anda (1984) make absolute sense; encouraging bilingualism, supplying translators, mediators, and models, giving corrective feedback, and teaching analytic skills.

Helping Recent Immigrants

The cultural model is also pertinent when working with new immigrants, including those from Asian, Latin American, and African societies. Immigrants differ from refugees in that they arrive voluntarily and are likely to come from industrializing, if not already industrialized, nations with a free market economy. Because present immigration laws favor individuals with needed occupational skills, many are likely to be educated with a working knowledge of English. Because of these things, cultural differences among immigrants is not likely to be as great as those among refugees.

The process of immigration, because it is a voluntary renunciation of previous citizenship, inclines people to identify with being American and therefore to biculturate, perhaps even assimilate, as quickly as possible. It is not surprising that research often finds that those who immigrate are different from those who do not. For instance, Koh and Bell (1987) found that elderly Korean immigrants were more educated, more likely to have a religious preference, and more likely to be Christian than their nonimmigrant counterparts. Similarly, in spite of no difference in the number of children they could count on for help, the Korean elderly in the United States were more likely to prefer to live in separate, independent households than their South Korean counterparts.

Be this as it may, social workers should still expect to find cultural differences at the center of the helping process with many new immigrants. New immigrants are not likely to be totally at home in American English and the children, spouses, and relatives that accompany them may not know English. Any number of private troubles can be related to the process of immigration or to the absence of complete knowledge about American cultural expectations. They may become quite ambivalent about their adopted homeland, and its values, as they begin to confront them on a daily basis. For instance, East Indian immigrants often bemoan the loss of traditional medicines, the loss of parental authority, and changes in the role of wife and mother (Jensen, 1980). Immigrants may also have some familiarity with social services, but they will not know how American social services function. Translators, mediators, models, problem-solving skills, and corrective feedback will undoubtedly form the basis of ethnic sensitive services.

Helping Minorities

The cultural model becomes less useful when thinking about helping clients from ethnic and racial groups who have been in the United States for generations yet who still find themselves in a minority status; African Americans in particular but also Native, Mexican, Puerto Rican, and to some extent, Japanese and Chinese Americans. It is less useful because so many within these groups were born and raised within the context of American institutions such that it is untenable to argue that the private troubles they experience stem from a lack of knowledge of the dominant norms and expectations or its opposite, a commitment to values and beliefs at odds with the dominant norms and expectations. Even the most physically isolated—those living on reservations, in inner-city ghettos, or in southwestern barrios—are affected by the norms and expectations of the larger American society. Contact with the schools, with the health and welfare systems, with the economy, with the political system, with the military, with religious, largely Christian, denominations, and with the omnipresent media daily provides models, translators, mediators, feedback and problem-solving skills the cultural model presumes are lacking.

This assertion of course has to be qualified. In the first place, immigration from abroad—both legal and not so legal is increasing the ranks of these groups: African Americans immigrating from Africa, Haiti, Jamaica and other parts of the West Indies; Mexicans from Mexico; and Puerto Ricans from the Island. Like any other immigrant, they will be in need of bicultural socialization. In the second place, internal migration is also taking place; African Americans moving from south to north and west, Native Americans moving from rural reservations to urban centers, Puerto Ricans moving from New York to the west and mid-west; and Mexican Americans moving from the southwest to the mid-west and northeast. Although internal immigrants generally speak English, and will have had considerable contact with American institutions, it is fair to assume that the process of change will require a certain degree of adaptation to different regional—if not national—expectations. In some instances, particularly among Native Americans from tribes located in remote rural areas, the adaptation will be akin to the experience of foreign immigrants. Yet for most others, adaptation to different norms and expectations will represent a tuning up rather than a complete overhaul.

Those, like de Anda (1984), who assert there are vast cultural differences between the Anglo majority and African, Asian, Native, Mexican, and Puerto Rican Americans born and raised in the United States woefully exaggerate their claims. Although de Anda is interested in the implications of cultural differences, it is curious that she never becomes specific about the vast differences she claims exists. Green (1982) and McNeely and Badami (1984) do attempt to become specific, and it is at this point we start to get uncomfortable with the cultural model.

Take for instance, Green's example of Hispanic health and illness beliefs. He writes as if most Hispanics held such beliefs yet the number of Hispanic Americans who hold the kind of beliefs about health and illness that he describes is probably quite small. In my own doctoral dissertation (Longres, 1970), completed almost twenty years ago, I found that rural Puerto Rican women—women who were quite isolated from mainstream Anglo American culture—were likely to abandon the use of folk medicine once exposed to public school education. In a recent study, Van Oss, Padilla, and De La Rocha (1983) interviewed a nonrandom sample of low-income Hispanics—the sector where these beliefs might be expected to be widespread—and found that 20% had used a *sobador,* 12% a midwife, 10% a *botanica,* 9% a *curandero,* and 6% a home or folk remedy for serious medical symptoms. Likewise, Keefe, Padilla and Carlos (1979), in two studies of randomly sampled Mexican Americans found—in the first—that only 2% had used a *curandero* in the last year and—in the second—that only 1% had ever used a *curandero.*

A study by Sharp, Ross and Cockerham (1980) also throws doubt on the generality of Green's claims about natural and unnatural illness among African Americans. Using a probability sample of Illinois residents, they found that African Americans had significantly more positive attitudes toward visiting physicians than did whites. They also found that African Americans were more inclined to believe that symptoms warranted a visit to a physician.

The same difficulties arise when examining the contributions of McNeely and Badami (1984). On the surface their observations ring true. On closer inspection they become suspect. Although they say they are comparing white and African American, inner-city, 16-year-olds, two of their examples describe the behavior of adults. They describe a new African-American high school teacher who, when a white staff person calls him by his first name, asks to be addressed by his title and last name and they describe a cocktail party where, instead of mingling, African American and white faculty form separate cliques each with a distinct atmosphere about it. As for young people, this practitioner has never met a white or African-American, rural or urban 16-year-old that insisted on being called by his or her last name. Nor for that matter have I worked with a 16-year-old, inner city, lower class, white youth who is trustful of authorities and prefers to learn from reading books rather than direct experience. More importantly, many of the behaviors McNeely and Badami describe attribute to cultural differences are better interpreted in terms of social class differences and situationally specific interracial conflict.

TOWARD A STATUS MODEL OF ETHNIC SENSITIVE PRACTICE

There are important differences in the behaviors of minority and majority group members. In terms of psychosocial well-being, it is clear that some social problems are more visible in minority groups than in majority group members. Minority status is often associated with poor economic and educational achievement, high rates of teenage pregnancy and single parenthood, high infant mortality, high criminal arrest rates, and high levels of drug and alcohol dependence. In terms of help seeking behavior, minorities are likely to see problems and their solutions differently from majority group members. And in terms of the helping relationship, it may very well be that minority group members are more likely to exhibit the kinds of behaviors McNeely and Badami observe: intermittent eye contact, insistence on formality, boastfulness, and distrust. But how should these behaviors be interpreted?

The cultural model assumes that behavior follows directly from values; the private troubles, help seeking behavior, and patterns of communication of minority group members are determined by the presence or absence of a particular group norm or value, or, as in de Anda's analysis, in terms of a failure in biculturation. As indicated, researchers have not documented the existence of vast group differences in attitudes and values. In addition, given the generations of experience with American social, economic, and political institutions,

it is unwarranted to conclude that there is widespread failure in biculturation among members of minority groups. Social workers need to
look beyond the culture of minority groups to explain private troubles,
help seeking behavior, and communication patterns. In this regard, the
concepts of *status* and *status differences* hold considerable promise.

Status refers to positions in a social hierarchy or stratification system. Social hierarchies are systems of inequality built around any number of dimensions (prestige, power, or wealth) and reflected in any
number of social institutions (economic, political or religious). Stratification systems emerge from social conflict, and although they give
order and stability to society, they also become a major impetus for
disorder and change. Groups at the bottom want to raise up while those
at the top want to hold on.

Ethnic and racial stratification systems are one type of status hierarchy clearly apparent in the United States. Our system shows up in
what we call the *dominant culture* in both its formal aspects—language, laws, and customs—and its informal aspects—whom we wish to
marry, be friends with, and live next door to. It arose from the military
conquest of Native Americans by Europeans and was built onto as
African Americans were forced to immigrate as slaves, as Mexican
territory was incorporated by military action, as Chinese were not
given the privilege of citizenship, and as southern and eastern Europeans voluntarily immigrated as free workers in search of the economic
opportunities not accorded slaves, Native Americans, Mexicans and
Asians. In the twentieth century, the conquest of Puerto Rico, and the
new waves of legal and illegal immigrants and refugees have continued
to shape the stratification system. As groups competed with each other,
the status hierarchy changed. Where northern and western Europeans
once dominated the United States, today the hierarchy is increasingly
embodied by a white majority group population at the top followed by
various minority group people of color. It is not surprising, therefore,
that de Anda (1984) must interrupt her cultural argument by noting—
almost as an afterthought—that physical features, the race factor, can
facilitate biculturation. What she really means is that, given the low
status of people of color, models, translators, mediators, problem-
solving techniques, and feedback have not so far been able to dent the
dominance of white Americans. By having to call attention to the importance of race, her argument about the failure of biculturation is
undermined.

The private troubles of minority group people of color are related
to the public issues of racial and ethnic inequality. When people look

across the generations and realize that their life chances are limited because of their color, what can we expect of their psychosocial well-being? We can expect them to have to struggle to meet basic human needs. Some struggle valiantly within the system, never giving up hope in their ability to succeed against all odds. Others organize to form voluntary associations in the hope of encouraging community development and social reform. But many get beaten down by what appears an impossible situation and begin to take advantage of illegal opportunities, live only for the moment, and participate in self and other destructive behaviors. These are the ones likely to become the clients of social service agencies. More often than not, they are forced into services involuntarily; something they did got them in trouble with authorities and they were court ordered or otherwise intimidated into service.

Very predictable things happen once minority people of color are clients in the social services; ethnic and racial conflict in the larger society get visited on the social work relationship, especially when the social worker is white. Minority clients are inclined not to trust workers and to be uncooperative. They come late, miss appointments, refuse to confide, keep their head and eyes down, become argumentative and manipulative, boast of their abilities, and insist that they be treated respectfully. They do not believe that services planned and delivered by members of the majority group, and perhaps even by minorities who have made it, can be trusted to help them.

Archibald (1976) has put forth a theory of expectable behavior in encounters between people of high and low status that sheds light, on the one hand, on the help-seeking and -receiving behavior of minority clients, and on the other hand, on the help-giving behaviors of majority workers. He argues that encounters between people of high- and low-status are always threatening and therefore must be adapted to. Most of the time, high- and low-status people try to avoid each other; they live in different neighborhoods, join different clubs and associations, go to different social activities, or just stay away from each other. When McNeely and Badami (1984) describe the behavior of white and African American faculty at a cocktail party they demonstrate avoidance behavior. When social service workers complain that minority clients miss appointments, come late, or drop out of service, they should not see cultural styles, they should see avoidance.

But sometimes, as in the case of encounters in the social services, high- and low-status people cannot avoid each other. When they do meet, Archibald argues, they do things that prevent the formation of an open and personal relationship; they relate on a very narrow, role-specific basis and try to control and manipulate each other. Not surprisingly, he points out that hostile feelings underlie a good deal of their interaction even though they go unexpressed most of the time.

Archibald's theory helps explain the observations of McNeely and Badami and are reinforced in the writings of others who have observed the interaction between whites and minorities of color. For instance, Lockart (1981) notes that because of a history of colonization and war, Native Americans carry around a strong distrust of Anglo Americans. This distrust shows up in the way Native Americans approach counselors; they suspect the advice that counselors give, fear their judgmental attitude, feel controlled by expectations of change, and manipulated by trying to get to the problem too quickly.

Similarly, De Lo and Green (1977) observe that many encounters between white and black are not "honest transactions . . . characterized by open and genuine communication" rather they are "dishonest transactions . . . characterized by a 'game' quality in which ultimately one or both individuals is 'put down' " (p. 296). In some transactions the white person manages to put the African American down, while in others the African American person puts the white down. In many transactions a stalemate occurs where both parties feel put down. The observation of McNeely and Badami (1984) about the learning preferences of African American and white youth may be reinterpreted in the light of dishonest transactions. They describe the following situation:

> During a classroom discussion . . . a white student states: "One of the studies says that white people. . . ." A black classmate interrupts: "Never mind what the book says—what do you think?" After offering a few generalities, the white declines to continue the exchange: Look, don't get so excited about it. It really doesn't matter that much . . ." (p. 23).

Does this example describe culturally based learning styles or does it describe dishonest communication where a low-status person has managed to intimidate a high-status person? I think the latter is a more accurate interpretation.

Another example is found in the work of Pierce (1970). He instructs on the offensive mechanisms used by white counselors to put down African American clients. He asserts that underlying most of these is the message that African Americans should be grateful and appreciative of all the help they are getting from a white person. Among the mechanisms used by whites are those that show false affection ("We love you blacks to death."), those aimed at bolstering one's own ego ("We're good to you blacks."), and those aimed at protecting the status of whites ("We whites are right.").

A final example shows that one need not be consciously offensive to subvert an honest discourse. Levy (1968) describes the degradation experienced by whites in the Civil Rights Movement of the 1960s. They joined because they sincerely wanted to help yet many operated on the assumption that they (whites) could be leaders in the African American movement. African Americans accepted them into the movement but as resources not as leaders; it was an African American movement to be led by African Americans. At first, the contentment that whites felt at being part of the movement shielded them from perceiving the mistrust that African Americans felt toward them. When they could no longer shield themselves, whites often became indignant insisting that they were not like other whites, they could be trusted to lead. Their contentment was soon gone, and they often became awkward and unsure of themselves. When they could not accept their role as one resource among many, they often left the movement in dismay.

It is important to emphasize that these examples are offered to show the effects of social status on human behavior. It would be wrong to take these as examples of personality problems, and certainly not as racial or cultural traits. It would also be wrong to minimize the effects of social status by thinking that a little sensitivity can overcome them. The history of race relations in the United States has produced enslavement, lynching, Jim Crow laws, genocide, reservations, deportation, internment in war camps, and Aryan nation marches. The privileges of high racial status are not given up easily. The disprivileges of low racial status race are not forgotten easily.

SUMMARY AND CONCLUSIONS

Ethnic sensitive models of social work practice are proliferating. The dominant model emphasizes differences in cultural norms and values; the problems experienced by people of different ethnic and racial groups, the way they seek and receive help, and the way they communicate are attributed to cultural beliefs or failures in biculturation. This model is extremely useful with clients who have recently entered the United States as refugees or immigrants but it is much less useful with minority clients. For African, Asian, Mexican, Native and Puerto Rican Americans who have been in the United States many generations it is not so much their culture that determines the way they respond to service but rather the subordinated position they find themselves in. For them, and the social workers who would help them, the helping encounter is a threatening one that encourages adaptation through avoidance, manipulation and hostility. If social workers are to be helpful, they need to spend less time thinking about differences in norms and values and more time thinking about how to operate in encounters between high- and low-status people. Helping minority clients means changing stratification systems.

REFERENCES

Archibald, W. P. (1976). Face to face: The alienating effects of class, status and power Divisions. *American Sociological Review, 41* 819–837.

Bogardus, E. S. (1968). Comparing racial distance in Ethiopia, South Africa, and the United States. *Sociology and Social Research, 52*(2), 152.

Bowen Wright, M. (1980). Indochinese. In S. Thernstrom (Ed.), *Harvard encyclopedia of American ethnic group.* pp. 508–513. Cambridge, MA: Belknap Press.

Green, J. W. (1982). *Cultural awareness in the human services.* (especially pp. 28–48) Englewood Cliffs, NJ: Prentice-Hall.

de Anda, D. (1984). Bicultural socialization: Factors affecting the minority experience. *Social Work, 29*(2), 101–107.

De Lo, J., and Green, W. A. (1977). A cognitive transactional approach to communication. *Social Casework, 58*(5), 294–300.

Handelman, Mark. (1983). Social workers as socializing agents. *Practice Digest, 5*(4), 3.

Jensen, J. M. (1980). East Indians. In S. Thernstrom (Ed.), *Harvard encyclopedia of American ethnic groups,* pp. 296–301. Cambridge, MA: Belknap Press.

Keefe, S. E., Padilla, A. M., and Carlos, M. L. (1979). The Mexican-American extended family as an emotional support system. *Human Organization, 38*(2), 147–148.

Koh, J. Y., and Bell, W. G. (1987). Korean elders in the United States: Intergenerational relations and living arrangements. *The Gerontologist, 27*(1), 68–69.

Lockart, B. (1981). Historic distrust and the counseling of American Indians and Alaska Natives. *White Cloud Journal, 2*(3), 31–34.

Longres, J. F. (1970). *Social conditions related to the acceptance of modern medicine among Puerto Rican women.* Unpublished doctoral dissertation. University of Michigan, Ann Arbor, MI.

McNeely, R. L., and Badami, M. K. (1984). Interracial communication in school social work. *Social Work, 29*(1), 22–26.

Pierce, C. (1970). Offensive mechanisms. In Barbour, F. B. (Ed.), *The black seventies,* pp. 265–82. Boston: Porter Sargent.

Sharp, K., Ross, C. E., and Cockerham, W. C. (1980). Symptoms, beliefs, and the use of physician services among the disadvantaged. *Journal of Health and Social Behavior, 24*(3), 255–263.

Van Oss Marin, B., Padilla, A. M., and De La Rocha, C. (1983). Utilization of traditional and non-traditional sources of health care among Hispanics. *Hispanic Journal of Behavioral Sciences, 5*(1), 65–80.

*This paper is
the revised version of
the Carl A. Scott Memorial Lecture
presented at the 37th Annual Program Meeting,
Council of Social Work Education,
March 1991, New Orleans, Louisiana.*

LEON F. WILLIAMS, PhD, is Associate Professor at the Boston College Graduate
School of Social Work.

REVISITING THE MISSION OF SOCIAL WORK AT THE END OF THE CENTURY: A CRITIQUE

Leon F. Williams

The author disputes many of the unexamined altruistic assumptions of the social work profession, noting its lack of progress in attracting minorities, its inattention to serious social needs, its backward-looking stance in terms of theory and intervention, and the market-driven nature of its educational and practice enterprises that ties the profession inexorably to a single-practice modality. He ends with a series of recommendations for social work education and practice that, if adopted, would assist the profession to become more universal in scope, more flexible in meeting new environmental demands, and more in touch with its traditional clientele and values.

SOCIAL WORK AND THE PUBLIC TRUST

A growing anger and resentment is apparent among minorities, among women, and among the underclasses that are associated with the hypocrisy, venality, and cynicism in high office that has so recently been the moral tone of the United States. This anger is reflected within the profession, especially as it is perceived that the mainstream of social work has drifted further and further into irrelevance in response to the current crisis. At this juncture in U.S. history, the growing backlog of societal wants and needs will assuredly have a profound impact on social work. It is assumed that this crisis, like similar crises in the past, will find the profession wanting. This is owed, in part, to the passive, bureaucratic, over-professionalized nature of the field that has evolved under a series of conservative administrations. As long as there is no public outcry against our practices (as is now the case in the professions of education, medicine, and law), we can contrive to sustain our collective denial for decades. Our public, experiencing economic recession and social despair, appears to be in no mood, at the moment, to examine social work closely. Nevertheless, the public does believe that our profession is accountable to the poor and disaffected.

Despite our rhetoric, a large share of the public and a sizable number of working professionals in our own midst believe that we ought to do more than we have and that we are off track. For the sake of high enrollments, and a large population of dues payers, we have allowed our profession to become a buyer's market. Student interests and circumstances dictate academic priorities—not vice versa (Wodarski, Pippin, & Daniels, 1988; Moore & Urwin, 1991). Moreover, faculty and curriculum resources have become skewed. Were it not for the administration and supervision courses, the macro part of the curriculum would wither away given the overwhelming number of students concentrating in clinical services (Butler, 1992; Rubin & Johnson, 1984). We no longer believe in the apprenticeship model—that infants should crawl before they walk and that social work role models are important to that process. We assume that two years of preparation, one of which is given over to general studies of the profession, is adequate to turn out a fully trained, *autonomous* professional; one who needs no further guidance from those senior to him or her. Alas, the beauty of professionalism is that it has a monopoly and that this monopoly can set its own standards. The professional monopoly, however, rests on the self-defeating logic of peer review that excludes all but insiders from the process of evaluating professional effectiveness, although the public pays. As a self-regulating but publicly sanctioned profession, social work is in far more danger from its complacency than from effectiveness. Complacency may find the field again, as in the 1930s and 1960s, leaving it unprepared for the onslaught of public ills that will demand immediate and innovative solutions from the profession.

In this half of the century, social work has fallen into certain habitual ways of thinking—ways of knowing and doing that have not been subjected to systematic scrutiny or critical analysis by other than those with a vested interest in seeing the field expand. As a consequence, there are a number of overarching beliefs that are assumed to be givens. Included among the profession's reigning assumptions are:

• We are doing useful and vital work.
• We have a vital interest in those less fortunate than ourselves.
• We have a commitment to diversity.
• We are a profession.
• We are a science-based profession.

We Are Doing Useful and Vital Work. The National Institute of Mental Health reported on a study that compared the roles of social work, psychology, and psychiatry in the mental health field, in the monograph the *Future of Mental Health Services Research* (1987). The study concluded that both social work and psychology served the easiest clientele in their practices and that the most difficult, trenchant cases were handled by physicians and psychiatrists (Knesper, 1987). Given the profession's lofty aims, and in view of the problems facing the lower half of our society—homelessness, poverty, neglect, and abuse—this is tantamount to an indictment. Advocates for the poor and oppressed can not work up much empathy for the profession in its current preoccupation with the personal adjustment problems of the more affluent classes.

An example of how far from the ideal and from the real the profession has strayed is contained in an incident reported in the *Boston Globe* (Blake, 1990). A mental health clinic in Boston reportedly complained that their traditional clients were being replaced by adult citizens who needed more concrete services, such as housing, health care, job counseling, and assistance with food and clothing. The agency professed discomfort with the shift in clientele. Accustomed to offering private psychotherapy to a more or less affluent middle class, the clinic was challenged to find out what to do with the needs of the ordinary citizen in recessionary times. One would suspect that what the applicants were responding to was a perception that social work and social agencies helped general categories of people. They had no way of knowing that social work was now helping particular people with particular problems. Incidentally, this clinic was threatened with closure because of drastic budget reductions in state mental health funding.

Part of the complaint by clinic personnel is symptomatic of the drift in the profession away from social work purposes and methodologies and into that uncharted territory of mental health professionalism. The basis of our uniqueness was in the practice wisdom developed over the years by social workers, and the foundation of that wisdom rested on our desire to simply be of help under a variety of conditions, using a variety of means (Siporin, 1982; Stewart, 1986). We lost our distinctive social work identity, and thus, we have lost our opportunity to further sharpen and strengthen our public image and acceptance as a vital factor in social development and change. Now, the public is confused and so are we.

One's work is not meaningful or useful unless there is a public demand for it. There was and is a demand for social work. What muddies the water is the blending of social work with other mental health professions. There is now a mental health system that has as its objective the marketing of psychological services rather than the responding to mundane needs. It reminds one of the position of modern advertising in that consumer demand for a product is created through advertising rather than on the intrinsic quality of a product. The developments in mental health over the years appear to have been primarily in marketing. By narrowing the definition of normal behavior, many human behaviors are now suspect that may not have been in the past, creating new fields and industries for psychological intervention. With broadened diagnostic categories in the DSM nomenclature, it seems we are turning trivial and routine stresses of living into pathologies for the purpose of profit. One has only to be reminded of the surge in popular psychological conditions, such as premenstrual syndrome (which has sexist implications); the emergence of depression as a global category that gives increased diagnostic latitude to the clinician; the myriad variations on the principle of codependency; posttraumatic stress disorder applied willingly well beyond its original reference group of Vietnam veterans; adults who were abused as children; persons with sexual addictions; and adult children of alcoholics and adults of other dysfunctional family situations. Few of these mental health statuses has other than anecdotal support for their elevation to the position of *critical social problems.* One would fondly hope that professionalism could require a basis, other than anecdotal to elevate new categories of human dysfunction—even when, and despite the fact that, there are groups of persons quite willing to provide personal testimony for any condition in intimate detail. Television is packed with people willing to be identified with the latest craze, who want to feel themselves psychologically unique, and who are quite willing to attest to the most intimate details of their lives to gain public attention.

We Have a Vital Interest in Those Who Are Less Fortunate Than Ourselves. One need not recap the litany of accusations that have been directed at social work over the past several years. It is instructive that there seems to exist an inverse correlation between the rise in the clinical-psychological movement in social work since the 1960s and in the reduced services to the poor and to persons of color, along with a decline in participation of MSW-trained social workers in the public or personal social services, whose clients include the most vulnerable groups. Something about the trends in the profession have taken it further from those least desirable clients, and we need to ask *why.* That we serve the *least desirable citizens* at all (those whose circumstances are defined by lower social status) seems more a function of randomness rather than any deliberate choice on our part.

We can not ignore these trends and expect to be in business very long. The demographic pool of middle-class, white people willing to partake of therapy is dwindling. The 1980s was the crest of a bubble. Although I must admit, as does Specht (1988), that the psychotherapies have opened up a whole array of well-paid and prestigious careers for social workers; especially those who are well-situated, married to a good source of referrals, fortunate enough to have the means to be a part of a private clinic in conjunction with others in the psychological professions (Specht, 1988). Conversely, in large measure, these opportunities have *not* emerged for minority professionals, requiring as they do an insider or mentoring relationship.

Specht predicts that the bubble of clinical entrepenurism will burst like our brief flirtation with community change in the 1960s and 1970s. I cannot believe that a new administration in Washington will allow social work to conduct business as usual in an atmosphere of chronic and rapidly growing social ills.

In the meantime, we are encouraging and recruiting students into our field with promises that may or may not lead to their professional survival. There are several questions we must ask and then answer— honestly. Why the rush of new recruits into social work after licensure? Who are our student bodies? A partial answer to both is instructive. New recruits are, or have been, older, working, white females seeking to become licensed psychotherapists (Specht, 1991), who are for the most part members of that generation typified by the media as the "me generation," and, with few exceptions, in their zeal for status may not have a clue about, nor patience for, the concerns of the profession (Josephson, 1990). We responded to this demand with innovations in academic programming so that now we offer courses on weekends, in extended part-time arrangements. The first year of training, especially the research and policy courses, and the introduction to the profession is sheer agony for many of these students. They are well-schooled but poorly educated; a paper is drudgery of the highest order, and we send them out to placements that infantilize them, while spoon feeding them cases too unimportant for the skilled technicians on site. This is especially true in conservative, psychodynamic environments. This trend follows them into their second and specialized year. With the advent of fee-for-services and liability statutes in some states, students may have far less access to real clients than ever before. So where are they getting these specialized skills that allow for post-MSW autonomous and unsupervised practice?

We have experienced an influx of more students committed to a single method, with schools skewing their resources and curricula to a method of dubious validity for a host of social problems (alcoholism, drug abuse, violence, teen parenting, poverty, and so forth). For the past twenty years, we have been cannibalizing the public agencies for student trainees, who do not elect to return to those agencies on completion of their degree. Why would they? They were not challenged during the course of their studies to see as noble work public services with the dependent, the frail elderly, the abused and neglected children, and the seriously mentally ill? The methods they were taught were restricted to a particular clientele and to circumscribed problems. The height of hypocrisy is then manifested in badgering students in their first year about their commitment to advocacy, to minorities, to social concerns, and to the poor and in releasing them subsequently in the second year to pursue their individual interests, which are more often than not in private psychotherapy.

Even if we could interest them in working with minorities and the poor, they would be ill-prepared for such practice by virtue of the fact that there is little room in tightly packed curricula for extraneous theoretical content directed toward practice with the poor and dependent. Currently, there is almost no room for electives. Even if space existed, the methods or applied courses would expand to fill the available vacuum.

We Have a Commitment to Diversity. In the early 1970s, the Council on Social Work Education and the National Association of Social Workers passed policies designed to eradicate racism and discrimination in the profession (Williams, 1981). Despite this commitment, schools have witnessed, in the last five years, little growth in minority student enrollment and level growth in minority faculty. The most critical fall off has been among minority males in all areas of the profession. The downward trend in minority enrollment, especially of targeted minority males, such as Puerto Ricans, Chicanos, African Americans, and Native Americans, identified by Rubin & Whitcomb (1978) have not reversed themselves in the 1990s (Lennon, 1991). Indeed, we share this experience with a number of academically based professions, but I find the issue critical in a profession that has been built on and has direct, historical ties to low-income and minority communities. With the loss of the social action thrust in the profession in the mid–1970s followed by the intense reactionary turn toward self-improvement and psychotherapy, a major factor that had drawn a number of African American males to the profession—social change —was no longer a cache of the profession. Social change simply vanished as a professional objective in favor of individual change and adjustment. With that came a change in the political posture of the profession (Wyers, 1991). It can be theorized that the clinical, private model that resulted is essentially passive rather than active, individualistic rather than group-oriented, pessimistic about change rather than optimistic—and atavistic. That is, a throw back to an earlier age dominated by white males, whose motives were inherently sexist and racist because their research and theories were tested and tried from the dominant perspective. These theories draw people away from the arenas of their oppression, turning them inward to self-doubt and blame.

A critical variable that would gauge the commitment to diversity in the profession is found in the representation of minority males, in particular, African American, Hispanic American, and Native American. A true commitment to diversity and social justice would have us seeking ways to restore a social action thrust within the profession that would, perforce, reawaken an interest among minority males in our profession—their presence or absence in significant numbers being a strong indicator of the diversity of the profession (Berger, 1989).

We Are a Profession. We must confront the fact that we are a profession in the making. Our interests are too varied and broad to constitute a corpus of knowledge that would distinguish us readily from other groups calling themselves professional. Our areas of expertise overlap so many other disciplines . . . sociology, psychology, medicine, education, nursing, psychiatry, and law. Despite the confusion and overlap, by fiat, we can, however, lay claim to a generally verifiable knowledge base and declare the objective of our practice to be autonomy. This latter idea was a stroke of genius. We managed to acquire a critical aspect of professionalism that also freed practitioners from supervision and public oversight, such as is found in the bureaucracy, and from having to be accountable in their practice to the least desirable client (Specht, 1991).

Even if none of what has been observed thus far is true, the critical failing of our so-called profession, it seems to me, is that of *universalism.* Most established professionals can say that they provide services to the public. If one is a physician, for example, his or her medical knowledge is (a) as valid working with the pygmies as with Scandinavians and (b) not limited by whether or not the person is underclass or upper-class. On the other hand, social work knowledge and skill seems more and more constrained by class factors, by age, by race, and by gender. We are just not very adept at providing services to people with characteristics other than being neurotic, female, white, and middle class.

We Are a Science-Based Profession. I have argued in the past and will argue now that what the profession owes clients is effectiveness and efficiency in its methods (Williams & Hopps, 1987); that what it does to and for them should be based on the best available knowledge. Those methods should stand the test of empiricism: They should work as they are said to work, and they should hold up under a variety of conditions. Despite arguments to the contrary, empiricism is like being from Missouri, you have to show me. It appears that just as social work arrived at the threshold of being truly accountable, of having methods that could effectively evaluate our practice, reaction has set in. We have witnessed a growing number of attacks on the empirical methods by social work educators and others (Dean & Fenby, 1989; Geismer & Wood, 1982; Heineman, 1981; Jayaratne & Levy, 1979). These authors, speaking as advocates of more humanistic approaches and adapting deconstructionist principles drawn from neoconservative thought, have given us qualitative research and single-subject research as paradigms that are supposedly more attuned to social work's existential needs. One can only be a skeptic when education adopts a single modality, such as N-of-one research, as a method of evaluating a complex and ever evolving practice. If one has appreciation for the mathematical and philosophical paradigms on which arguments for reliability and validity rest, qualitative designs are fraught with serious danger for objectivity.

What is troubling about the debate is that it seems to come at just the right time to deflect the profession from its goal of accountability. We must note that no research alternatives have surfaced that yields the kind and quality of knowledge that we have acquired about the profession as that created by quantitative means and scientific methods (Thyer, 1989). Note also, that at a time when we have created a cadre of home-grown minority researchers capable of asking (and answering) hard questions about the effectiveness of social work in working with their communities, one gets these philosophical and diversionary debates. Given the complexities of their problems, ethnic minorities require the best care from the most knowledgeable and sophisticated practitioners. In a related manner, these groups also require better studies with more powerful multivariate tools that can illuminate the causes of poverty and homelessness, disentangle the web of institutional racism and oppression, and target practice effectiveness with at-risk populations—not angels on pins arguments questioning the epistemological correctness of the profession's thought structure.

Unfortunately, the profession's paternalism, or maternalism, is showing: In the past, to retain a math-phobic population of applicants, we have sought to make the research requirements easier. We dropped the thesis, limited mathematically based reasoning is expected; although some schools are reviving comprehensive exams and research-based reports, they are no longer standard fare. We are generally left with single-subject design research as a palliative for the applied aspect of research theory. It would appear that the unspoken purpose has been to make research palatable to people who are not likely to use it in their practice. Given trends in society, research must be a part of every social worker's stock in trade. It can act to screen out those with frivolous interests in the field. If they are motivated to become social workers, they will get it. It is a method for disciplining the process of understanding experience. If used correctly, scientific research has built into it safeguards that control the natural tendency to project onto reality whatever we want it to be for our own purposes. Quality, objective research rids us of class and ethnic interests and frees us from our prejudices and from the limits of our observations (Hoover, 1984; Williams & Hopps, 1988). Until we can field highly trained empirical practitioners, we will not reach the ideal of a science-based profession.

SUMMARY

Social work has a challenge ahead—that is, to reclaim the profession for its own ends. It appears to have lost its identity and purpose in the generalized field of mental health. As a consequence, it has become one with a host of mental health professions—whose ends are fee-for-service in the marketplace. We should revive in the profession a concern for and capability of working with the least desirable citizen, the poor and oppressed populations, not because these groups demand it, but because these services are what defines social work and makes it unique. In the future, high-quality professionalism (exemplified by caring, well-trained, scientifically oriented, compassionate, and universal professionals) should become central to the education, training, and practice of social workers. Accreditation has not assured us quality in training, and licensing has not ensured it in practice (Williams, 1981). Quality is assured by satisfied consumers and by public sanctions.

The only way I can find to pursue my agenda is to begin with our academic training institutions, the gatekeepers. As Stewart (1986) notes, our graduate schools, more than ever responsive to student-consumer demands to the practice community, have abdicated leadership in determining the prerequisites for producing truly educated graduates. Just as often, they tend to follow trendy, and often superficial, practice approaches. Many faculty, disparaging of and ambivalent about their own social work heritage (many of whom come out of practices so specialized that their identity with the field is questionable) contributed to blurred identities on the part of students. In too many instances, schools produce technicians rather than professional social workers. In conclusion, we have also lost the sense of cause in social work and our mission as advocates, as social and political activists in behalf of the oppressed and dependent (Stewart, 1986, p. 45).

Given what has been argued thus far, my wish list of policies intended to preserve what is inherently just and equal in social work education (and thus the profession) would be to have the profession adopt the following guidelines as a backdrop for future policy:

- Retain at all costs the two-year, full-time requirement for the MSW degree and focus on the quality of socialization, mentoring and role-modeling that goes on among part-time students. Loosening up this criteria has accelerated the process whereby students have become alienated from the profession and its obligations to the poor and dependent. (Although previous research has found little difference between full-time and part-time students, anecdotal evidence from a variety of faculty suggests that perhaps our instruments may not be picking up the true variations (see Yamatani et al., 1986; Frumkin, Grigsby, and Granger, 1981)). Out of expediency, education will have to continue to provide a part-time option for the moment, but it should be under strict guidelines that would enhance the student's socialization into the values and purposes of the profession.
- Consider the concept of dual methods and eliminate the tendency toward specialized and, thus, technical training. One can envision a requirement of two methods, one in the micro realm and the other in the macro realm, with a minimum of nine credits in research.
- To preserve the diversity that comes from universalism, require every student to have at least one practicum experience working with a race or culture other than his or her own. If local agencies cannot

provide such, schools should move to create cross-cultural practicum centers led by school-based faculty, if necessary.
* Hold out the title of *social worker* to mean only those persons with the background and training of a full-fledged professional social worker, capable of providing leadership in, and working with, a variety of groups under a variety of circumstances. Those who elect a subspecialization not clearly identified with social work, such as clinician or planner, should be asked to complete a third year with the final internship in a minority practice setting.

In addition to these guidelines, when the profession recognizes a salient and significant social problem, it should have a way to marshal its resources to focus on the problem, such as communicating concerns to schools of social work and to agencies and directing them to bring their resources to bear on the problem. Currently, a significant social problem, which will perhaps find its way into the academic system in another decade, is the problem of African American males, their health, their oppression, and their alienation. Schools face a singular challenge in assisting this group through advocacy; recruitment and retention as students and practitioners; research and scholarship into their plight; and the creation of practice curricula content specific to their needs.

And furthermore, through accreditation, the Council on Social Work Education should move to clear up the ambiguity in its diversity statutes. Programs are required to address the needs of special populations, ethnic minorities, oppressed groups, as well as of groups defined by gender and sexual orientation. This has led to strains and tensions, pitting one group against another, creating general confusion. The result has been that many programs are doing nothing more than "papering over" the issue of diversity by adding lines to bibliographies and syllabi that faculty do not teach and students do not read. It is perfectly obvious that the profession must ultimately reserve its energies for the most vulnerable, at-risk populations. These are populations to which societal reaction is so perverse as to threaten their very lives and well-being. Generations of these groups may vanish, may be impaired beyond redemption, or may suffer so grievously as to enrage the sensibilities of normal citizens.

In general, the profession needs a new approach to diversity. Diversity should not become an end in itself blinding us to the ills of a race-based and class-ridden system of rewards and entitlements. Nor should it mean a smorgasbord of all the divisions of humankind. It should be defined precisely by those groups who are oppressed and at-risk within a multicultural context. We can assume that oppression manifests itself in historical and regional variations. All groups are not subject to *direct* oppression for all time. For example, the Japanese among the category of Asians, the African American and Hispanic *professional* classes, and the non-Marielito Cubans in Miami are all examples of groups that have survived their initial oppression and *now have the wherewithal to actively resist.* They cannot be considered endangered groups when weighed in the balance of the serious risks confronting the pariah classes. Yet, the former groups continue to gain advancement based on the general case for discrimination and endangerment.

At-risk groups vary regionally, as well. The oppression of gays is probably more extreme in rural America than in San Francisco. In other words, groups at-risk in one region may not be so in another. As a result, in my formulation, schools would be accountable for at-risk and unempowered groups in their local population, should the profession move so far as to make this a standard for accreditation purposes. Beyond local groups at-risk are groups and populations that transcend region and time: the poor, the African American (particularly male) and Hispanic underclasses, and lower class women among other groups who can be named and identified. All schools ought to provide coverage of these oppressed groups in their curriculum and research. This eschews the mere passive study of these groups or the use of these subjects in student training laboratories, but mandates that schools take an active posture toward them that is designed to change their circumstances. Call it liberation or call it economic and political justice, schools (and agencies) should marshal their resources and influence to advocate for change, to research and highlight, and to bring socio-political pressure to bear in behalf of these populations.

Indeed, such a reformulation would take into account the fact that groups will appear and reappear on any list of at-risk populations, as society, the law, and the profession responds or fails to respond to their needs. To cite but two examples: When historical and regional variables are taken into account in curriculum and program decisions, one school may find it necessary to include content on and give special attention to Vietnamese immigrant problems and culture (in coastal Texas), while another program might choose to focus on the homeless, on the severely mentally ill, or on single parents. These programs would or could establish research centers, pilot programs, conduct field studies, and establish cooperative practice in high-risk communities, while marshaling resources in an active effort to eradicate the problems confronting those groups. It would produce some genuinely unique educational institutions with missions and purposes that might elevate many of them above the mediocre, as defined by standards for accreditation. A rational, caring body such as our profession should not voluntarily submit to the dissonance that is now called *social work practice.* Social work has to find a way to return to preeminence in the fight for social justice. It is time to turn disaster into a moral, cultural, and intellectual renaissance. There is no penalty for thinking but a dear price to pay for not acting. A whole generation of young minorities are being sacrificed to the politics of race, class, and economic expediency. We need a change, a new purpose, a new direction, even if it means tampering with our vainglorious illusions.

REFERENCES

Blake, A. (1990, Oct. 25). Local mental health agencies hit hard by state deficits. *Boston Globe,* p. 30.

Berger, R. (1989). Promoting minority access to the profession. *Social Work Education, 34*(4), 346–349.

Butler, A. C. (1992). The attractions of private practice. *Journal of Social Work Education, 28*(1), 47.

Dean, R., & Fenby, B. (1989). Exploring epistemologies: Social work action as a reflection of philosophical assumptions. *Journal of Social Work Education, 25*(1), 46–54.

Frumkin, M., Grigsby, K., & Granger, B. P. (1981). Alternative social work education: Status, issues and directions. *Journal of Continuing Social Work Education, 1*(4), 11–15.

Geismer, L., & Wood, K. (1982). Evaluating practice: Science as faith. *Social Casework, 63,* 266–272.

Heineman, M. (1981). The obsolete scientific imperative in social work research. *Social Services Review, 55,* 371–397.

Jayaratne, S., & Levy, R. (1979). *Empirical clinical practice.* New York: Columbia University Press.

Josephson, M. (1990 Nov. 11). Sex, lies and the 'I deserve-it' generation. *Boston Globe,* p. A18.

Hoover, K. R. (1984). *Elements of scientific thinking.* New York: St. Martin's Press.

Knesper, D. J. (1987). Substitution in production as the basis for research and policy relevant to mental health specialists. In C. A. Taube, D. Mechanic, & A. A. Hohmann (Eds.) *The future of mental health services research* (pp. 63–80). Rockville, MD: National Institute of Mental Health.

Lennon, T. M. (1991). *Statistics on social work education in the United States: 1991.* Washington, DC: Council on Social Work Education.

Moore, L. S., & Urwin, C. A. (1991). Gatekeeping: A model for screening baccalaureate students for field education. *Journal of Social Work Education, 27*(1), 9.

Popper, K. (1972). The sociology of knowledge. In J. E. Curtis & J. W. Petras (Eds.), *The sociology of knowledge: A reader,* p. 651. New York: Praeger Publishing.

Rubin, A., & Johnson, P. J. (1984). Direct practice interests of entering MSW students: Changes from entry to graduation. *Journal of Education for Social Work, 20,* 5–16.

Rubin A., & Whitcomb, R. G. (1978). *Statistics on social work education in the United States: 1978.* New York: Council on Social Work Education.

Siporin, M. (1982). Moral philosophy in social work. *Social Services Review, 56,* 518–531.

Stewart, R. P. (1986). Social work practice in mental health: Accomplishments, failings, strategies for the future. In W. Buffum (Ed.) *Charting the future of social work,* p. 31–52. Houston: University of Houston, Graduate School of Social Work.

Specht, H. (1988). *New directions for social work.* New York: Prentice Hall.

Specht, H. (1991). Should training for private practice be a central component of social work education? No! *Journal of Social Work Education, 27*(2), 102–107.

Thyer, B. A. (1989). Letter to the editor in response to Dean & Fenby. *Journal of Education for Social Work, 25*(2), 174–176.

Williams, L. F. (1981). *Indices of institutional racism: A survey of non-discriminatory practices and educational quality.* Ann Arbor, MI.: University Microfilms International.

Williams, L. F., & Hopps, J. (1987). Publication as a practice goal: Enhancing opportunities for social workers. *Social Work, 32,* 373–376.

Williams, L. F., & Hopps, J. (1988). On the nature of professional communications: Publication for practitioners. *Social Work, 33*(5), 453–459.

Wodarski, J. S., Pippin, J. A., & Daniels, M. (1988). The effects of graduate social work education on personality, values, and interpersonal skills. *Journal of Education for Social Work, 24*(3), 266–277.

Wyers, N. L. (1991). Policy-practice in social work: Models and issues. *Journal of Education for Social Work, 27*(3), 241–250.

Yamatani, H., Page, M., Koeske, G., Diaz, C., & Maguire, L. (1986). A comparison of extended and traditional master's of social work students: A repeated measures analysis. *Journal of Social Work Education, 22*(3), 43–51.

*This paper is
the revised version of
the Carl A. Scott Memorial Lecture
presented at the 38th Annual Program Meeting,
of the Council of Social Work Education,
March 1992, Kansas City, Missouri.*

*It is based on
Dr. Ozawa's articles,
"Basis for income support of children: A time for change" and
"Unequal treatment of AFDC children by the federal government,"
both written in 1991 in
Children and Youth Services Review, 13, 7–27 and 257–269,
respectively, with permission of the Pergamon Press, Ltd.*

MARTHA N. OZAWA, PhD, is the Bettie Bofinger Brown Professor of Social Policy at the Washington University George Warren Brown School of Social Work.

INEQUITY IN INCOME SUPPORT
FOR CHILDREN

Martha N. Ozawa

While the United States needs to make all adults on Aid to Families with Dependent Children (AFDC) a part of the productive labor force, it also needs to support children on welfare adequately and to plan to make them part of the next generation of productive workers. The Family Support Act of 1988 (P.L. 100–485) attempted to meet the first objective, but not the second. Thus, the author addresses the problem of categorical and geographic inequities in income support for children by comparing trends in benefit levels for children on social security versus those on AFDC and by examining the state-by-state differences in the federal subsidies for AFDC payments. She concludes that the federal government should institute a national minimum payment for AFDC or that Congress should pass the once-failed Fiscal Federalism and Partnership Act that would have provided near-poverty line benefits to all AFDC families. In the long run, the federal government should address the income needs of children more directly by instituting refundable tax credits or children's allowances.

Across the nation, both in government and industry, policymakers are searching for answers to the American dilemma: the need for the country to become economically competitive and to deal with both the low birthrate and the aging population. With the American economy changing rapidly and becoming increasingly technological, these policymakers are trying to ensure a viable work force to meet the demand for highly skilled workers in the coming decades.

The Family Support Act of 1988 (P.L. 100–485), a welfare reform measure, was passed in this environment. No longer could policymakers consider Aid to Families with Dependent Children (AFDC) to be an income maintenance program that would provide eligible families with a certain level of income for an extended period. Rather, they began to view the AFDC as a transitional program that would channel AFDC mothers into the American labor force—not out of a sense of generosity or charity, but out of the shear need to protect the national interest (Vosler & Ozawa, 1988). To make our economy competitive again, policymakers needed to make all Americans more productive, including AFDC mothers. Hence, the most important component of this law is the nationwide welfare-to-work program—the Job Opportunities and Basic Skills (JOBS) training program. Under this program, participating AFDC mothers are given educational and manpower training and are provided with transitional assistance in child care and health care for one year after they leave the welfare rolls.

Thus, a clear redirection of welfare policy seems to be in place. The Family Support Act, however, fell short of addressing the future of children growing up in welfare families. Although the Act provided for stronger enforcement of child support by noncustodial fathers and for increased funding for states to provide JOBS participants with child care in the form of direct care, cash, or vouchers, these provisions were not directly concerned with the long-range objective of making AFDC children part of the next generation of productive American workers. The purpose of strengthening the enforcement of child support was to save taxpayers money, and the aim of the child care provision was to help AFDC mothers find and keep jobs. In short, though revolutionary in many respects, the Act dealt with only half of the agenda: making AFDC parents a productive part of the labor force. It neglected to develop a policy on behalf of children who grow up in low-income families, especially those in AFDC families.

Unlike most of the industrialized societies, the United States has never directly provided income support to children. Instead, it has provided indirect support, depending on the work status and earnings level of their parents. Moreover, the United States has not yet established a national floor of income support for children as it did for the elderly. The lack of a U.S. policy on income support for children has created both categorical inequity and geographic inequity. With categorical inequity, children are treated differently, depending on the degree of their parents' attachment to the labor force. Children of parents who have worked and thus are eligible for social security benefits receive adequate support, whereas children of parents who have not worked receive inadequate support through public assistance programs. With geographic inequity, different amounts of AFDC payments are provided, depending on where the children reside.

In light of the urgent need to develop a national policy on investing in the future generation of children, these inequities seem counterproductive. It is imperative that policymakers search for a better way to intervene on behalf of the nation's children. Thus, the investigation of the federal government's role in financing AFDC seems particularly relevant at this juncture, as the public searches for a national policy on children.

In addressing the problem of categorical inequity and geographic inequity in income support for children, in regard to categorical inequity, one should ask: How differently do Social Security and AFDC programs treat children? What benefits do they provide? What is the trend in children's benefits in these two programs? What is the justification for such an inequity? What is the rationale for change?

In regard to geographic inequity, one should ask: Through its subsidization of AFDC, how much money does the federal government pay to AFDC children, depending on where they live? Why do such differential federal subsidies exist? How did the federal government's unequal treatment of AFDC children come about?

CATEGORICAL INEQUITY: CHILDREN ON SOCIAL SECURITY VERSUS THOSE ON AFDC

Trends in Levels of Benefits

The fate of children who receive income support from the government is determined by the degree to which their parents are attached to the labor force and by the social hazards that the parents encounter, such as old age, disability, or death. Thus, the amount of income support that children receive from Social Security and AFDC is determined by a two-stage differentiation (a) whether or not, and the degree to which, their parents have worked, and (b) the reason why their parents stopped working, for example, old age, disability, or death.

Figure 1 presents the average monthly benefit for children under Social Security during the period 1960–1989, and Figure 2, under AFDC. AFDC payments for children equaled the average payment per recipient.

The striking difference in the trend in average payments under the Social Security and AFDC programs is that Social Security benefits for children have increased considerably over the years, while AFDC payments for children have not. During the period 1960–1989, the average monthly benefit for a retired worker's child increased 94 percent; for a disabled worker's child, 21 percent; and for a deceased worker's child, 79 percent. In contrast, the average benefit for each child under AFDC increased during the latter half of the 1960s, stabilized during the

FIGURE 1. Average amount of monthly Social Security benefit for children, 1960–1989 (in 1989 dollars).

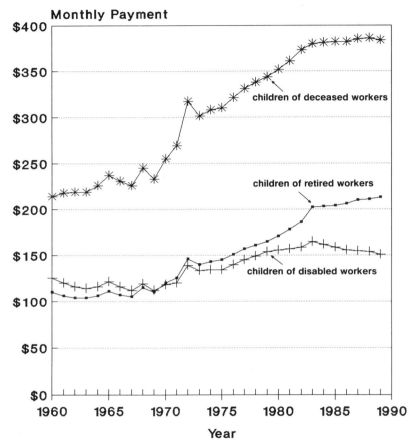

Sources: Social Security Bulletin: Annual Statistical Supplement, 1990 (Washington, DC: U.S. Social Security Administration, 1990), Tables 5C, 5E2, and 5F6, pp. 185, 193, and 198; *Statistical Abstract of the United States,* 1991 (111th ed., Washington, DC: U.S. Government Printing Office, 1991), Table 770, p. 478.

FIGURE 2. Average amount of monthly AFDC payment for children, 1960–1989 (in 1989 dollars).

Note: Equal to the average amount of monthly AFDC payment per recipient.

Sources: Statistical Abstract of the United States, 1991 (111th ed., Washington, DC: U.S. Government Printing Office, 1991), Table 770, p. 478; *1991 Green Book: Background materials and data on programs within the jurisdiction of the Committee on Ways and Means* (Washington, DC: U.S. Government Printing Office, 1991), Table 21, p. 620; *Social Security Bulletin: Annual Statistical Supplement, 1975* (Washington, DC: U.S. Social Security Administration, 1975), Table 177, p. 187.

1970s, and then started to decline in 1978. The decline subsided in 1982, making the average benefit stable once again. As a result, the average monthly AFDC payment in 1989 was only 11 percent higher than in 1960.

The consistent increase in Social Security benefits for children is attributed to three factors: First, benefit levels were increased legislatively in 1968, 1969, 1970, and 1972 and have risen automatically since 1974 because of cost-of-living increases. Second, Social Security programs have matured—that is, covered employees have had the opportunity to contribute to the Social Security system throughout their working lives—resulting in a steady increase in benefits under Old-Age Insurance (OAI) and Survivors Insurance (SI). Third, reflecting the general growth in average wages until the 1970s, later cohorts of beneficiaries received higher benefits than did earlier cohorts. Because children on Social Security nominally receive a percentage of the primary insurance benefits (their parents' benefits)—75 percent under SI and 50 percent under OAI and Disability Insurance (DI)—children's benefits have increased as their parents' benefits have increased for these three aforementioned reasons.

In recent years, benefits for children who are covered under DI have been subjected to a series of laws that have been enacted to (a) determine more strictly the number of "dropout" years in averaging monthly earnings, (b) coordinate DI benefits with benefits under workers' compensation and other disability-related public programs, and (c) define the maximum family benefit for the disabled worker's family more strictly than for retired or deceased workers' families (Social Security Administration, 1981).

Compared with the trend in benefits for children on Social Security, the trend in AFDC payments for children has been haphazard and subjected to the political climate of the time. In all states except California, benefit levels have failed to keep pace with inflation. The median decline in the benefit level (maximum payment for a family of three with no income of its own), adjusted for inflation from 1970 to 1991, was 42 percent (U.S. House of Representatives, Committee on Ways and Means, 1991, p. 603).

As of 1989, the average monthly AFDC benefit was lower than the benefit paid to any category of children on Social Security. In comparing the level of children's benefits under Social Security and under AFDC, one can make a fair comparison only between children's benefits under SI and children's benefits under AFDC. Under both circumstances, the family can have only one parent at home, whereas children on OAI or DI can have two parents. Furthermore, the parent beneficiary on OAI or DI receives at least twice the amount that each child receives, but AFDC payments for children and their mothers are assumed to be the same.

The comparison of SI benefits for children with AFDC payments for children indicates that children on SI are in a much better financial condition than are children on AFDC. In 1989, for instance, the monthly average benefit for a child of a deceased worker was $384, compared with $131 of AFDC.

The relative disadvantage of children on AFDC is more pronounced than what these figures project. If a mother on AFDC earns a certain amount, AFDC benefits for the entire family may be cut off. Under SI, the earnings of the surviving spouse (the parent of the children) do not lower the benefits of surviving children. Instead, if the surviving spouse earns enough to be taken off the Social Security roll, benefits for each surviving child may increase because the surviving, working spouse, who does not receive survivors' benefits, will mitigate the negative impact of the rule of maximum family benefits on the benefits that each surviving child receives (Social Security Administration, 1986). Furthermore, the family on Social Security can own an unlimited amount of assets without their benefits being affected, while the AFDC family cannot.

Justifications for Categorical Inequity

As the United States faces the challenge of nurturing all children to their full potential, what explains the institutional inertia in treating children differently according to their parents' work experience and the social hazards their parents face? Does such differential treatment of children make sense in the rapidly changing economic and demographic circumstances of this society?

The original framers of the Social Security and public assistance programs paid close attention to the differential treatment of the programs' recipients. They thought that the levels of Social Security benefits should be tied to previous earnings and that only those who contributed to the Social Security system should be entitled to benefits. Furthermore, to claim benefits from the Social Security system, they believed that the insured worker should have had encountered statutorily defined social hazards that include old age, disability, or death, but not desertion, divorce, or nonmarriage. Benefits for the worker's children were to be a percentage of the worker's benefits: the higher the worker's benefit, the higher the child's benefit (Altmeyer, 1968). The framers of these programs also thought that applicants for public assistance should fall into recognized categories—the elderly, the disabled, or children of deceased or incapacitated fathers—with the determination of payment levels for public assistance left up to the states (Altmeyer, 1968). After all, they believed, the role of public assistance would wither away as the Social Security system became fully implemented or matured (Garfinkel & McLanahan, 1986).

Even the objectives of the two types of programs were perceived differently: The framers believed that the objective of the Social Security programs was to prevent poverty and that of public assistance programs, to relieve poverty (Garfinkel & McLanahan, 1986). In short, public assistance programs were considered the ultimate, residual measure to assist families on a stopgap, transitional basis.

Furthermore, the framers had an ideological basis for legitimating the differential treatment of families on Social Security and those on welfare. They believed that families on Social Security earned their benefits through contributions and that families on welfare, instead, should be at the mercy of the public's willingness to hand out assistance. Thus, families on welfare had no right to question the level of assistance, the framers believed.

The public's and policymakers' resistance to increasing AFDC payments has been closely tied to their belief in the work ethic. In a basically noncoercive society, such as the American, the only way to ensure that the great majority of people will choose work over nonwork is to treat those who are in or had been in the labor force more favorably than those outside the labor force. Thus, it was thought, earned income through work has to be higher than public assistance payments, and those who have worked must be treated better in the system of income maintenance as well. Consequently, social insurance programs, such as Social Security, have to provide higher payments than do public assistance programs. In conclusion, different levels of payment for Social Security and AFDC epitomize the ideological stance that this society has taken to sustain the value attached to work (Ozawa, 1982b).

The categorically different treatment of adults—those on Social Security versus those on public assistance—is basic to the American economic system's commitment to free enterprise, to individual thrift and effort, and to reward and punishment based on individual merit (Heclo, 1986; Ozawa, 1986). The common denominator in this system is the extent of the individual's attachment to the labor force and the extent of his or her economic contribution.

In a culturally diverse society such as the American, many think that such a system of reward and punishment makes good sense because the individual—and hence society—can prosper as a result. If American society was stratified by caste on the basis of occupation, as in Japan until the 19th century; on birth, as in India; on religion, as in many parts of the Middle East; or on race, as in South Africa, the United States would never have been united politically nor economically—because it would have been plagued by constant fights over who should deserve more economic rewards than should others. The rules of the game that derive from the work ethic make it easy for everyone to understand why some are treated better than are others. Of course, this system of economic rewards has never been practiced in a completely fair manner in the United States. In particular, discrimination against minorities, especially African Americans, taints the long-believed credo of economic free enterprise. Nonetheless, the belief in this economic system has been the driving force behind the establishment of the system of income maintenance in the United States.

It is important to remember, however, that children suffer because of their parents' treatment in this American economic game plan and that their economic well-being is dictated by how their parents fare. Thus, a major question that needs to be raised is this: Given the changing economic and demographic circumstances of the United States, does it make sense to ignore the need to establish a public policy on the basic economic well-being of children with the objective of maintaining the social contract between society and its adult population? Put another way, is the United States not loosing by not dealing directly with the basic economic well-being of children?

Rationale for Change

Given the well-ingrained ideology surrounding the concept of work and the concomitant rationale for treating adults differently in the American income maintenance system, it is difficult to develop a counterideology and a counterrationale for treating children any differently from the way they are treated today. The current ideological stance and the rationale of the programs are simply too entrenched to make a breakthrough. One can offer, however, several pragmatic reasons why the United States can, and should, change the way it treats children.

The public generally thinks that the provision of children's Social Security benefits, which are a percentage of the workers' benefits, is part of the insurance scheme; it believes, thus, that the formula used to calculate children's benefits cannot be changed. That belief, however, is far from the truth. Because the amount of Social Security taxes does not vary according to the number of children a worker has, the eventual benefits for children are justified only on the basis of the principle of social adequacy—the welfare objective. They do not reflect the principle of individual equity that is tied to the concept of insurance. That is, only the worker's (the parent's) benefits—not the child's—adhere to the principle of individual equity. Thus, children's Social Security benefits reflect society's values and desires at a given time; they are not an inherent right of the insured worker-parent. Once one reasons this way, the line between children's Social Security benefits and children's AFDC payments wanes, indeed; and it becomes clear that it is up to the public to decide how it wants to treat children–both those on Social Security and those on welfare.

In addition, the provision of benefits to children on Social Security that are a percentage of their parents' benefits is not a universal practice. For example, the Japanese social security system provides flat-amount benefits to children (except the first surviving child in the absence of the surviving spouse, who receives a proportion of earnings-related benefits in addition to flat-amount benefits) and does not have the rule of maximum family benefits (Ozawa, 1991). Canada follows a similar rule (Social Security Administration, 1988). Thus, the formula to calculate benefits for children can be changed according to the judgment of the government. If, for instance, flat-amount benefits for children are instituted, children of low-wage earners would be favored. The elimination of the rule of maximum family benefits would favor beneficiaries with a large number of children, among whom nonwhites are overrepresented.

There is no inherent reason why children on Social Security should be provided with higher benefits than should children on other income-support programs. For example, Japan provides a higher level of benefits to children under its Child Support Allowance program and its Special Child Dependent's Allowance program than under its social security system (Ozawa, 1991). (The Child Support Allowance program provides income to children in female-headed families, while the Special Child Dependent's Allowance program provides income to disabled children.)

Furthermore, there is no inherent reason why children of insured workers should be treated separately from other children. West Germany, for example, has recently eliminated children's benefits from social security and consolidated them under its child allowance program (Social Security Administration, 1988).

The foregoing discussion indicates that depending on the value judgment of the public and of policymakers, there is room to consider the development of a more general policy to address the income needs of all children without categorizing children according to the backgrounds of their parents. Likewise, it becomes possible to break down the barrier against increasing AFDC payments for children.

GEOGRAPHIC INEQUITY IN FEDERAL SUBSIDIES FOR AID TO FAMILIES WITH DEPENDENT CHILDREN

Development of the Scheme for Federal Subsidies

Since the inception of AFDC in 1935, then the Aid to Dependent Children (ADC) program, the federal government's role in subsidizing the program has been passive. Although the law spelled out procedural guidelines for the administration of the AFDC, it left the decision about the benefit level with the states.

Because the AFDC deals with both the economic dependence and the social deviance of recipients (Handler, 1972), the level of AFDC payments in a state reflects not only the state's ability to pay, but also the taxpayers' sense of the appropriateness of the payment level and their willingness to tax themselves—that is both the economic and the political conditions in the state. As a result, the payment levels vary widely among the states—and not necessarily according to a particular state's ability to pay or the cost of living in the state. For example, as of January 1991, Alabama provided a maximum payment of only $124 to a three-person family with no income, compared with $694 in California and $891 in Alaska (U.S. House of Representatives, 1991, pp. 604–605).

The federal subsidy comes into play only when a state's AFDC payments are determined. In particular, the federal share of a state's AFDC payments is determined by the matching formula specified for Medicaid in Title XIX of the Social Security Act. Before the federal share is determined, the state's share is calculated as follows:

$$\text{State's share} = \frac{(\text{state per capita income})^2}{(\text{national per capita income})^2} \times 45 \text{ percent}$$

Then, the federal government's share is calculated as follows:

Federal share = 100 percent − the state share

(with a mininum of 50 percent and a maximum of 83 percent).

The second formula indicates that the maximum subsidy rate that a state can expect is 83 percent and the minimum rate, 50 percent. For example, 79 percent of Mississippi's AFDC payments are subsidized by the federal government, in contrast to 50 percent of California's AFDC payments.

State-by-State Comparison in Federal Subsidy

Table 1 shows the average monthly federal subsidy for AFDC payments per recipient, the average monthly AFDC payment per recipient, the subsidy rate (e.g., the federal government's share), the per capita personal income in the state, and the percentage of African Americans in the state for the 10 lowest and 10 highest states, ordered according to the amount of federal subsidy they receive. (The federal subsidy is calculated by multiplying the average monthly AFDC payment by the subsidy rate.)

As Table 1 shows, in 1987, the monthly federal subsidy per AFDC recipient ranged from $28 in Alabama, to $107 in Vermont, and $114 in Alaska. States that received small subsidies, such as Alabama and Mississippi, generally had high subsidy rates. The reverse was also true. Among the bottom 10 states in federal subsidies, 5 states were subsidized at a rate greater than 70 percent. In contrast, among the top 10 states, only one state (Utah) was subsidized at a rate greater than 70 percent.

The amount of federal subsidy is smaller for states that provided lower monthly AFDC payments. Alabama, which received a federal subsidy of $28 per recipient, paid $39 per recipient per month. In contrast, Alaska, which received a federal subsidy of $114 per recipient, paid $228 per recipient. In general, the lower the AFDC payment in a state, the smaller the federal subsidy. This generalization also can be made by contrasting the ranking of federal subsidies with that of AFDC payments. There is a close parallel between the two.

TABLE 1. *States with 10 Lowest and 10 Highest Federal Subsidies for AFDC Payments, 1987 (per recipient)*

State	Average		Subsidy Rate (%)	Personal Income (per capita)	Percentage of African Americans (1980)[a]
	Federal Subsidy	AFDC Payment			
Alabama	$28 (50)[b]	$39 (50)	72	$11,940 (43)	25.6 (5)
Mississippi	31 (49)	39 (49)	79	10,292 (50)	35.2 (1)
Texas	31 (48)	56 (46)	55	13,866 (33)	12.0 (17)
Louisiana	36 (47)	55 (47)	66	11,473 (47)	29.4 (3)
Tennessee	38 (46)	54 (48)	70	12,880 (36)	15.8 (11)
Nevada	41 (45)	82 (40)	50	16,366 (12)	6.4 (26)
Arkansas	46 (44)	62 (45)	74	11,507 (46)	16.4 (9)
Florida	47 (43)	84 (37)	56	15,584 (17)	13.8 (13)
South Carolina	48 (42)	66 (44)	72	12,004 (42)	30.4 (2)
Delaware	49 (41)	98 (29)	50	16,696 (9)	16.2 (10)
Maine	84 (10)	124 (16)	68	13,954 (31)	0.3 (48)
Utah	85 (9)	116 (21)	73	11,366 (48)	0.6 (43)
Rhode Island	86 (8)	155 (10)	55	15,555 (18)	3.0 (34)
Michigan	87 (7)	153 (11)	57	15,393 (19)	13.0 (15)
Minnesota	91 (6)	172 (4)	53	15,927 (13)	1.3 (41)
Massachusetts	92 (5)	183 (3)	50	19,142 (3)	3.8 (29)
Wisconsin	93 (4)	162 (7)	58	14,742 (22)	3.8 (28)
California	95 (3)	190 (2)	50	17,821 (7)	7.7 (21)
Vermont	107 (2)	159 (8)	67	14,302 (27)	0.2 (50)
Alaska	114 (1)	228 (1)	50	18,230 (4)	3.5 (31)

[a] Percentage of African Americans in state based on 1980 U.S. census.
[b] Rankings set in parentheses.

Sources: U.S. House of Representatives, Committee on Ways and Means, *Background material and data on programs within the jurisidiction of the Committee on Ways and Means* (Washington, DC: U.S. Government Printing Office, 1988), Tables 16 and 19, pp. 421–422 and 426–427; U.S. Bureau of the Census, *Statistical Abstract of the United States: 1989* (Washington, DC: U.S. Government Printing Office, 1988), Table 701, p. 433; U.S. Bureau of the Census, *Statistical Abstract of the United States: 1984* (Washington, DC: U.S. Government Printing Office, 1983), Table 37, p. 36.

Poor states tend to receive small federal subsidies for AFDC payments. For example, Alabama, which received the smallest federal subsidy, was the 43rd state in terms of per capita personal income in 1987. Similarly, Mississippi, which received the second smallest federal subsidy, was the poorest state. In contrast, Alaska, which received the largest federal subsidy, was the fourth richest state. The ranking of per capita personal incomes generally runs in the same direction as the ranking of federal subsidies, although there are several deviations.

A relatively clear, inverse relationship is seen between the amount of federal subsidy and the percentage of African Americans in a state. That is, states with a high percentage of African Americans receive small federal subsidies. For example, Alabama, whose population was 25.6 percent African American according to the 1980 census—the fifth highest percentage in the nation—received the smallest federal subsidy. Similarly, Mississippi, which had the highest percentage of African Americans (35.2 percent), received the second lowest federal subsidy. All the bottom 10 states, in terms of federal subsidy, had relatively high percentages of African Americans, ranging from 6.4 to 35.2 percent. In contrast, all the top 10 states had relatively low percentages of African Americans, ranging from 0.2 percent to 13 percent.

These descriptive statistics show that there is a discernible pattern in the distribution of federal subsidies for AFDC payments. Larger subsidies go to states that provide high payments, to rich states, and to states with low percentages of African Americans. The reverse is also true. A multiple regression analysis was performed to investigate if this pattern has statistical significance.

Regression Analysis

To determine if the distribution of federal subsidies for AFDC follows a discernible pattern with statistical significance, the average federal subsidy per recipient was regressed on the per capita personal income, percentage of African Americans, tax effort, and birthrate in the states.

Tax effort is defined as the percentage of personal income that is collected in the form of all types of state taxes (U.S. Bureau of the Census, 1988, pp. 22, 280, and 433). It is calculated according to the following formula: per capita taxes collected by the state/per capita personal income × 100.

Birthrate is defined as the number of registered births per 1,000 population in the state (U.S. Bureau of the Census, 1988, p. 63). The 1987 data were used to formulate all the variables in the regression model, except the percentage of African Americans in the state and the state's birth rate, for which data from the 1980 census and from the 1986 vital statistics, respectively, were used (U.S. Bureau of the Census, 1983, p. 38; 1988, pp. 22, 63, 280, 433; U.S. House of Representatives,

TABLE 2. *Multiple Regression Analysis of the Federal Subsidy and the Average Monthly AFDC Payment, 1987*

	b Coefficients (Standard errors in parentheses)	
	Federal Subsidy	AFDC Payment
Intercept	−347.77*	−1,397.51***
	(118.42)	(192.62)
Per capita personal income (in log)	93.24**	346.30***
	(27.71)	(45.07)
Percentage of African Americans in state	−1.190***	−1.870***
	(0.235)	(0.382)
Tax effort	4.346**	8.812**
	(1.412)	(2.296)
Birthrate	0.313	1.534
	(1.060)	(1.723)
N	50	50
Adjusted R^2	0.519	0.698
F	14.236***	29.312***

* $p < .01$; ** $p < .005$; *** $p < .0001$.

1988, pp. 421–422 and 426–427). Per capita personal income in the state is expressed in the value of a natural logarithm.

Table 2 shows that all the independent variables except birthrate are significantly related to the average federal subsidy per recipient in the predicted directions. The states with a higher per capita personal income receive significantly more federal subsidies than do the states with a lower per capita personal income ($p < .005$). States that have larger percentages of African Americans receive significantly lower subsidies than do states with lower percentages of African Americans ($p < .0001$). States with higher taxes than others tend to receive higher federal subsidies ($p < .005$). The birthrate is not related to the amount of federal subsidy—that is, when the other variables are held constant, the states' birthrates do not make a difference in the amount of federal subsidy states receive. All told, the regression model explains 52 percent of the variance in the dependent variable, with an F ratio of 14.236 ($p < .0001$).

Table 2 also presents for comparative purposes the regression re-sults of the state's average monthly AFDC payments. The results indi-cate that federal subsidies for AFDC are related to the independent variables in much the same way as are the average AFDC payments. In particular, the states that have high per capita personal incomes tend to provide higher AFDC payments than do the states with low per capita personal incomes ($p < .0001$). States that have a high percentage of African Americans tend to pay lower AFDC payments than do states with a low percentage of African Americans ($p < .0001$). High-tax states provide higher AFDC payments than do low-tax states ($p < .005$). The birthrate is not related to the amount of AFDC payments that a state pays. All the independent variables together explain 70 percent of the variance in the dependent variable, with an F ratio of 29.312 ($p < .0001$).

The regression results of federal subsidies for AFDC and of AFDC payments signify that the distributional pattern of federal subsidies is similar to that of the AFDC payments themselves. The well-to-do states receive more federal subsidies and provide higher AFDC pay-ments than do the less well-to-do states. The states with a high concen-tration of African Americans receive less federal subsidies and provide lower AFDC payments than do the states with a low concentration of African Americans. The high-tax states receive more subsidies and provide higher AFDC payments than do the low-tax states.

How Did Differential Subsidies Occur? Are They Fair?

The regression results for AFDC payments are nothing new. Ear-lier studies reported similar findings (Collins, 1967; Ozawa, 1978). The regression results of federal subsidies, however, are bound to raise pol-icy questions. How has the federal government come to subsidize AFDC in such a way as to create such a pattern of the distribution of subsidies? Is such a distribution fair?

As was already mentioned, the federal government has been a passive partner in financing AFDC. The states have had the power to decide the payment levels; the federal government has only provided a percentage of the cost of the actual AFDC payments made by the states. The circumstances under which the Social Security Act of 1935 was developed and pushed through for Congressional passage forced the federal government to subsidize the states' AFDC programs through grants-in-aid, instead of direct financing. At that time, the constitutionality of the federal provisions under the Act was in doubt. The Supreme Court had already declared two child labor laws to be unconstitutional: one dealing with the right of the federal government to regulate interstate commerce and the other, with the taxing power of the federal government. The only social legislation that the Court had held to be constitutional by that time was the federal grants for states to finance maternity and child health programs (*Massachusetts v. Mellon,* 1923). Thus, the Roosevelt Administration had to be cautious in finding a way to participate in financing ADC that could withstand a possible court battle for its constitutionality. The only program under the Social Security Act of 1935 over which the Roosevelt Administration took the chance of having a constitutional battle was OAI. The Administration believed that only the direct financing and administration of OAI could ensure the portability of wage records and the continuity of the program (Altmeyer, 1968).

In addition, President Roosevelt believed that ADC should be a residual program and should eventually wither away. He said: "Work must be found for able-bodied but destitute workers" and "the federal government must and shall quit this business of relief" (quoted in Altmeyer, 1968, p. 16).

In light of the constitutional issue surrounding the provisions under the Social Security Act and the philosophical stance that the Roosevelt Administration took with regard to ADC, the grant-in-aid was the logical approach for the federal government to take in participating in the financing of ADC. Under grant-in-aid, it is up to the states to decide the level of benefits and even to decide to accept or refuse federal subsidies.

What is most relevant (for the purpose of this article) is the way in which the grant-in-aid has been implemented. Either under the original, matching formula or under the Medicaid formula that superseded the original one, the federal government has attempted to help states with less fiscal capability more than states with a greater fiscal capability. Thus, under the Medicaid formula (which is currently used for all the states), the federal share is determined by a formula that takes into account a state's per capita income in relation to the national per capita income. Since the variation in AFDC payments among the states has been so great, however, the apparently progressive matching ratios have resulted in smaller subsidies, in absolute terms, for poorer states than for richer states. As has been shown, Alabama, for example, was subsidized at the rate of 72 percent in 1987, yet received only $28 per recipient in federal subsidies; in comparison, Alaska was subsidized at the rate of 50 percent, yet received as much as $114 per recipient. As a matter of fact, because the difference in AFDC payments in these two states is so great, even if the federal government subsidized Alabama's AFDC payments at the 100 percent rate, the subsidies would still be vastly different. Furthermore, even if the cost-of-living differentials were taken into account, the difference in the subsidies would still remain.

Which states are subsidized more than are others? Are federal subsidies distributed fairly? This issue boils down to whether one takes a proportional view or an absolute view in assessing the extent of federal subsidies for the states' AFDC payments. If one looks at the subsidy rate, one tends to believe that the federal government helps poor states more than rich states. But if one measures the federal subsidies in terms of absolute dollars, then one concludes that the federal government helps rich states more than poor states.

Which argument makes sense: the proportional argument or the absolute argument? The use of an analogy to federal subsidies for Social Security benefits may help answer this question. (A subsidy is the portion of Social Security benefits that is not accounted for by the retiree's past contributions plus interest.) Under OAI, the Social Security benefits of high-wage retirees are subsidized proportionally less than are the Social Security benefits of low-wage retirees; however, the subsidies for high-wage retirees are greater in absolute terms than are those for low-wage retirees (Burkhauser, 1976; Ozawa, 1974, 1982a). Elsewhere, the author argued that there is no inherent reason why the federal government has to subsidize Social Security benefits according to how well workers fared in the world of work before retirement (Ozawa, 1982a). She further argued that after the federal government returns past contributions and interest in the form of Social Security benefits, it has no obligation to differentiate the amount of subsidies it provides to retired workers. For these reasons, the absolute argument in evaluating subsidies for Social Security benefits was advocated.

Applying the analogous argument to the situation of federal subsidies for AFDC, one can argue that the attempt to subsidize AFDC payments, on the basis of a percentage of the states' AFDC payments, is inherently unfair for poor states. Even if the matching ratio is slanted in favor of poor states, as it currently is, the attempt to subsidize the states' AFDC payments by using such a ratio—while the amount of AFDC payments is determined by the states—cannot produce nearly equal levels of subsidies to all states. Put another way, the apparently progressive federal matching formula is producing unequal subsidies, with poor states receiving less and rich states receiving more.

More importantly, as was shown earlier, a state's AFDC payments are related not only to the state's ability to pay but also to its racial composition and tax efforts. Thus, although the matching formula is determined solely by an economic variable (per capita income in the state in relation to the national per capita income), the AFDC payments for which the subsidy rate is applied are affected not only by the economic variable, but by the racial variable (the racial composition of the state) and by the political variable (tax efforts). Thus, the seemingly straightforward matching formula is applied to a state's AFDC payments, which are a product of the state's idiosyncrasies, as well as of the state's ability to pay.

The following example highlights the price that AFDC children in many states pay for such idiosyncrasies. Imagine two states with the same level of per capita income, tax effort, and birthrate, but with vastly different percentages of African Americans—in one state African Americans constitute 30 percent of the state population and in the other, 5 percent. On the basis of the results of the regression analysis shown before, one could expect hypothetically that the state whose population is 30 percent African American would receive $29.75 less in the form of federal subsidies per recipient than would the state whose population is 5 percent African American, although the matching ratio would be the same for the two states. This unfair distribution of federal subsidies occurs because the state with 30 percent African Americans has, on average, AFDC payments that are $46.75 lower than does the state with 5 percent African Americans (also estimated from the regression results) and then the same matching ratio is applied to differential AFDC payments in these two states. This illustration shows that because the federal government is only a passive partner in financing AFDC, it has inadvertently created the situation under which AFDC children in states with a high concentration of African Americans receive significantly smaller subsidies from the federal government. Much the same observation can be made with regard to the effect of tax efforts on federal subsidies: The federal government provides significantly smaller subsidies to AFDC children in low-tax states.

The foregoing discussion indicates that the original constitutional issue notwithstanding, the federal government is taking an inappropriate and ineffective approach to ensuring a minimum economic well-being for children who grow up in welfare families. The current demographic and economic conditions in this country are vastly different from those in the 1930s when AFDC was originated. Given U.S. challenge of facing international competition and of supporting an increasing number of elders, the federal government's method of subsidizing AFDC seems to be creating a distributional effect that is contrary to what should be the national goal: to nurture all children to their maximum potential. Currently, more subsidies are going to rich states than to poor states, to states with a low concentration of African Americans than to states with a high concentration of African Americans, and to states with high taxes than to states with low taxes. With a greater national interest in children emerging as indicated by the report by the National Commission on Children (1991), the fact that these factors are influencing federal subsidies for the nation's welfare children seems counterproductive. A new approach to federal involvement in financing AFDC seems to be in order.

WHERE DO WE GO FROM HERE?

Originating from the American work ethic and from the state's prerogative to set the payment standards for public assistance, it is evident that the current schemes of income support for children are treating the nation's children unfairly. Categorical inequity and geographic inequity in income support for children seems detrimental to the national interest.

What direction should the federal government take to minimize, if not eliminate, such inequity?

One option is to institute a national minimum payment for AFDC. The federal government could do so in a similar way to which it introduced a national minimum level of benefits for the elderly by implementing in 1974 the Supplemental Security Income program that was established by the 1972 amendments to the Social Security Act (P.L. 92–603). Another option is for Congress to again attempt to pass the Fiscal Federalism and the Partnership Act, which did not pass in 1987. This Act would enable the federal government to ensure nationwide minimum benefits that are pegged to poverty thresholds and would ensure both equal AFDC payments and an equal matching ratio in all states (U.S. Congress, Congressional Budget Office, 1989).

Under either option, the benefit level should increase to account for economic growth, as well as for inflation. The time for the government to intervene directly on behalf of the nation's children has come: The long-range income policy for children should go beyond increasing AFDC payments. In the future, children should not be provided with different levels of income support according to their parents' backgrounds nor according to the states' racial composition, political ideology, and ability to pay. Rather, it should reflect the society's need to invest in children and its assessment of what is required for children's optimal growth and development. Children's allowances, refundable tax credits for children, the provision of pre- and postnatal care and medical services for all children, and the provision of services and equipment for disabled children will naturally become the prototype of such income support programs.

REFERENCES

Altmeyer, A. J. (1968). *The formative years of social security.* Madison: University of Wisconsin Press.

Burkhauser, R. V. (1976). Are women treated fairly in today's social security? *The Gerontologist, 19,* 242–249.

Collins, L. S. (1967). Public assistance expenditures in the United States. In O. Eckstein (Ed.), *Studies in the economics of income maintenance* (pp. 97–174). Washington, DC: Brookings Institution.

Commonwealth of Massachusetts v. Andrew W. Mellon, 262 U.S. 447 (1923).

Family Support Act of 1988, 42 U.S.C. §1305.

Garfinkel, I., & McLanahan, S. S. (1986). *Single mothers and their children.* Washington, DC: Urban Institute Press.

Handler, J. F. (1972). *Reforming the poor: Welfare policy, federalism, and morality.* New York: Basic Books.

Heclo, H. (1986). The political foundations of antipoverty policy. In Sheldon H. Danziger and Daniel H. Weinberg (Eds.), *Fighting poverty: What works and what doesn't.* Cambridge: Harvard University Press.

National Commission on Children. (1991). Beyond rhetoric: A new American agenda for children and families. Washington, DC: Author.

Ozawa, M. N. (1974). Individual equity versus social adequacy in Federal Old-Age Insurance. *Social Service Review, 48,* 24–38.

Ozawa, M. N. (1978). An exploration into states' commitment to AFDC. *Journal of Social Service Research, 1,* 245–259.

Ozawa, M. N. (1982a). Who receives subsidies through social security, and how much? *Social Work, 27,* 129–134.

Ozawa, M. N. (1982b). Work and social policy. In Sheila H. Akabas and Paul A. Kurz-
man (Eds.), *Work, workers, and work organizations: A view from social work.* Engle-
wood Cliffs, NJ: Prentice-Hall.
Ozawa, M. N. (1986). The nation's children: Key to a secure retirement. *New England
Journal of Human Services, 6*(3), 12–19.
Ozawa, M. N. (1991). Child welfare in Japan. *Social Service Review, 65,* 1–21.
Social Security Act of 1935, IV A U.S.C. § 401.
Social Security Administration. (1975). *Social Security Bulletin: Annual Statistical Sup-
plement, 1975.* Washington, DC: Author.
Social Security Administration. (1981). Social Security disability amendments of 1980:
Legislative history and summary of provisions. *Social Security Bulletin, 44*(4),
14–31.
Social Security Administration. (1986). *Social Security handbook, 1986* (9th ed.). Wash-
ington, DC: Author.
Social Security Administration. (1988). *Social Security programs throughout the world—
1987.* Washington, DC: Author.
Social Security Administration. (1990). *Social Security bulletin: Annual Statistical Sup-
plement, 1990.* Washington, DC: Author.
U.S. Bureau of the Census. (1983). *Statistical Abstract of the United States: 1984* (104th
ed.). Washington, DC: U.S. Government Printing Office.
U.S. Bureau of the Census. (1988). *Statistical Abstract of the United States: 1989.* (109th
ed.). Washington, DC: U.S. Government Printing Office.
U.S. Bureau of the Census. (1991). *Statistical Abstract of the United States: 1991.* (111th
ed.). Washington, DC: U.S. Government Printing Office.
U.S. Congress, Congressional Budget Office. (1989). *Fiscal Federalism and the Partner-
ship Act of 1987.* Washington, DC: U.S. Government Printing Office.
U.S. House of Representatives, Committee on Ways and Means. (1988). *Background
materials and data on programs within the jurisdiction of the Committee on Ways
and Means* (100th Cong., 2d sess.) Washington, DC: U.S. Government Printing
Office.
U.S. House of Representatives, Committee on Ways and Means. (1991). *1991 Green
Book: Background materials and data on programs within the jurisdiction of the
Committee on Ways and Means.* (102d Congress., 1st sess.) Washington, DC: U.S.
Government Printing Office.
Vosler, N. R., & Ozawa, M. N. (1988). An analysis of two approaches to welfare-to-work.
New England Journal of Human Services, 8(4), 15–21.